Sylvia's
Soul Food

Sylvia's Soul Food

Recipes from Harlem's World-Famous Restaurant

SYLVIA WOODS and CHRISTOPHER STYLER

Hearst Books

New York

It is the policy of William Morrow and Company, Inc., and its imprints and affiliates, recognizing the importance of preserving what has been written, to print the books we publish on acid-free paper, and we exert our best efforts to that end.

Library of Congress Cataloging-in-Publication Data

Woods, Sylvia (Sylvia Pressley)
    Sylvia's soul food : recipes from Harlem's world-famous restaurant/
Sylvia Woods and Christopher Styler.
       p.   cm.
    Includes index.
    ISBN 0-688-10012-0
    1. Afro-American cookery.   2. Sylvia's Soul Food (Restaurant)
I. Styler, Christopher.   II. Title.
TX715.W895   1992
641.59'296073—dc20   92-16524
                                                                            CIP

Printed in the United States of America

First Edition

                    7   8   9   10

BOOK DESIGN BY GIORGETTA BELL MC REE

FOOD STYLING BY SARAH GREENBERG

It is with great love and lots of beautiful memories that I dedicate this book to my mother, Julia Pressley. She not only taught me how to cook, she showed me the way of life.

In loving memory of my brother McKinley Preston and my sister Louise Thomas, you will remain in my heart forever.

Acknowledgments

I am forever grateful to my husband, Herbert D. Woods, for his love, support, and companionship.

To my four children: Van, Bedelia, Kenneth, and Crizette, for the joy, happiness, and partnership that they bring to this family and to the business, and to all my wonderful grandchildren and great-grandchildren.

Special appreciation and thanks to my chef and lifelong friend Ruth Gully, who helped make this book a reality. Ruth, you hold a special place in this book and my life.

To all my staff and to all the wonderful people who have ever worked for me and with me to help make Sylvia's Restaurant a success. Thank you so much.

Special thanks and love to my four sisters-in-law: Mary, Bertha, Frances, and Willie; to Olga, Rebecca Cooper, and Sadie Frazier; and to our agent, Bill Adler, who made it happen.

Many thanks to Chris Styler for putting our years of work into words.

My special and loving friend Gael Greene. Thank you so much for introducing Sylvia's Restaurant to the media and the world.

My profound love and gratitude to my great customers: Thank you for not standing behind me, but for standing beside me through the years. I truly hope that you have enjoyed this relationship as much as I have.

Contents

Introduction

I was born and raised on my family's farm in Hemingway, South Carolina. My father, Van Pressley, died when I was only three days old, so it was under the loving, generous guidance of my mother, Julia Pressley, that I learned to respect hard work and pursue the things I wanted in life.

I graduated from cosmetology school, married my husband, Herbert, and ran my own beautician business in Hemingway while raising a young family. When I was in my twenties, Herbert and I moved to New York with our children.

Although I'd been cooking at home since I was a child, I had never even set foot in a restaurant until I got a job waitressing at Johnson's Restaurant in Harlem to help support our family. I had no experience—I didn't even know how to work the coffee urn—but Mr. and Mrs. Johnson were kind enough to let me stay on and learn the business. I had been working at Johnson's for eight years when Mr. Johnson decided to sell his business. To my great surprise he asked if I wanted to buy the restaurant. With our savings and the help of my mother, Herbert and I bought the restaurant in August 1962, and the following year we renamed it Sylvia's.

In those days it was a tiny place with only a few booths, but through hard work and with the help of our loyal staff and customers we did well. Sylvia's became so popular that in 1968 we moved a few doors down to our present location on Lenox Avenue and 126th Street, and we continued to grow as a popular neighborhood restaurant.

In 1979 *New York* magazine's restaurant critic Gael Greene wrote an article about us, and as the saying goes, "The rest is history." As a result of her review, we began attracting media attention and customers from all over the world, and I was crowned "the queen of soul food." Today, visitors from everywhere come to Sylvia's to sample our hearty soul food—from our famous fried chicken and ribs to our smothered pork and salmon croquettes, all served with traditional side dishes.

Our restaurant is a family affair—Herbert takes care of the shopping and building, and our four children—Van, Kenneth, Bedelia, and Crizette—all help out in the restaurant. Ruth Gully, also from Hemingway, has been cooking her delicious food in our kitchen for nearly twenty-five years and is assisted by her son Richard. In 1992, we celebrated our thirtieth anniversary and opened up a jazz and blues club next door to the restaurant called Sylvia's Also.

While running the restaurant has taken a lot of hard work, I'm doing what I love best—seeing to it that my customers are well fed and enjoying themselves. Visitors frequently ask me how they can prepare our dishes at home, so with the help of Chris Styler I finally wrote down our most popular recipes.

If you've been to Sylvia's, I hope you'll come again; if not, I hope you'll stop by soon. In the meantime, enjoy our traditional soul food at home with this collection of our favorite recipes.

Sylvia Woods

Sylvia's
Soul Food

Breakfast at Sylvia's

Biscuits

MAKES ABOUT 24 BISCUITS

During breakfast at Sylvia's these incredibly light and fluffy biscuits are eaten just about as fast as Ruth can make them. Making great biscuits like Ruth's might take a few practice batches. Once you're happy with the outcome, remember what the dough feels like—this will help you make perfect biscuits every time.

These biscuits are great for dipping in gravy, topping with preserves or syrup (page 3), or just eating plain.

½ cup solid vegetable shortening, plus more for the pan	4 teaspoons baking powder
5 cups all-purpose flour	2 teaspoons salt
½ cup sugar	1¼ cups milk
	4 large eggs

1. Preheat the oven to 400°F. Grease an 11- by 7-inch pan with shortening.

2. Stir the flour, sugar, baking powder, and salt in a large mixing bowl until blended. Make a well in the center of this dry mixture and add the milk, ½ cup shortening, and eggs. Mix the wet ingredients with your hands until the eggs and milk are blended. (There will still be some lumps of shortening.) Slowly work the dry ingredients into the wet ingredients with your fingertips. The finished dough should be soft but not sticky, so you may have to add a little more flour if it seems too wet, or stop mixing before all the flour is added if it seems too dry.

3. Turn the biscuit dough out onto a lightly floured surface. Roll the dough out to ½ inch thick. Cut into 3½-inch rounds and place side by side on the greased baking pan. (The biscuits should be touching but not overlapping.) Reroll the dough as many times as necessary to cut all the biscuits possible. Let the biscuits rest in a warm place 10 to 15 minutes (on top of the warm oven is a good place).

4. Bake until the biscuits are deep golden brown and light to the touch when you pick one up, about 20 minutes. If some of the biscuits are browning more quickly than others, rotate the pan after about 10 minutes. Break apart and serve.

■ ■ ■

Syrup and Biscuits

MAKES ABOUT 24 BISCUITS

The simplest things are often the best. In this case biscuits warm from the oven are topped with a little butter and drizzled with cane syrup for a homey and satisfying breakfast.

Cane syrup is made from ribbon cane, the first type of sugarcane grown in the States. The stalks of the ribbon cane are stripped and milled for sugar. The stripped stalks are then boiled to make this rich but not too sweet syrup that's used in baking and for toppings. Many larger supermarkets carry cane syrup.

1 recipe Biscuits (page 2)
1 cup (2 sticks) unsalted butter (at room temperature), or as needed

1 cup Cane-patch cane syrup, or as needed

Make the biscuits and, while they're still warm, split them and spread them with a little butter. Drizzle cane syrup on top of the butter and eat the biscuits right away.

■ ■ ■

Hotcakes

MAKES 8 SERVINGS

Nothing beats a stack of fluffy pancakes for breakfast. These are best piping hot right off the griddle, so feed your breakfast crew one at a time and settle in last with a plate of your own.

4 cups all-purpose flour
¾ cup sugar
2 tablespoons baking powder
2 cups milk
8 tablespoons (1 stick) unsalted butter OR margarine, melted, plus more for the griddle

1 large egg
2 teaspoons vanilla extract
½ teaspoon yellow food coloring

1. Stir the flour, sugar, and baking powder in a large bowl until mixed. In another bowl, beat the milk, melted butter, egg, vanilla, and food coloring until blended. Pour the wet ingredients into the dry ingredients and beat until just blended (it's better to leave a few lumps than to overmix and make tough hotcakes). The hotcakes will be lighter if you let this batter stand at room temperature for about 30 minutes, or refrigerate it up to 1 day.

2. Heat a griddle or large heavy pan (cast-iron is perfect) over medium heat. The griddle is hot enough when a drop of water skitters quickly across the surface. Brush the griddle with a little melted butter. Pour about ⅓ cup of batter for each hotcake, leaving a little space between the hot-cakes to make it easy to turn them. Cook them until golden brown underneath (lift a corner to peek) and bubbles start to pop on the topsides. Flip the hotcakes carefully and cook them until the undersides are golden brown. Repeat with the rest of the batter. Serve hot with butter and maple syrup.

Pork Breakfast Sausages

MAKES 8 SERVINGS

Nothing beats the flavor of home-ground pork breakfast sausages. These are peppery and well seasoned with cloves and sage. Whether you're using an electric or hand-cranked meat grinder, the sausages will come out better if all the parts of the grinder and the seasoned meat are well chilled before grinding.

2 **pounds fresh pork meat from the ribs, backbone, and sides (see the Note)**
1 **tablespoon crushed red pepper flakes**

2 **teaspoons rubbed sage**
2 **teaspoons salt**
1 **teaspoon freshly ground black pepper**
1 **teaspoon ground cloves**

1. Trim any gristle and connective tissue from the pork or the meat won't grind properly and the sausages will be tough. Cut the meat and fat into 1-inch cubes. Sprinkle the seasonings over the pork and toss to mix. Cover the seasoned pork and refrigerate at least 1 hour or up to a day.
2. Grind the meat in a well-chilled manual or electric meat grinder fitted with the medium disk.
3. Shape the sausage into 1½-inch balls, then press them flat to form patties ½ inch thick. Place half the patties in a large heavy skillet over medium-low heat. Fry until golden brown on both sides and no trace of pink remains in the center, about 15 minutes. Drain on paper towels. Repeat with the remaining patties.

Note: When buying the pork, ask the butcher to select cuts that are three-quarters lean and one-quarter fat. If that's not possible, have the butcher add some pork fat or very lean meat as necessary.

■ ■ ■

Grits

MAKES 6 SERVINGS

Breakfast wouldn't be breakfast at Sylvia's without a side order of snowy white grits. Serve the grits with a pat of butter and some Brown Gravy (page 29), if you like.

3 cups water	1 tablespoon salt
1½ cups white (*not* instant) grits	

Heat the water to boiling in a large saucepan over medium heat. Pour in the grits very gradually, stirring the whole time to prevent lumps. Add the salt, reduce the heat to low (one or two bubbles should rise to the top at a time), and cook, stirring constantly, until tender, about 10 minutes. Grits should be as thick as oatmeal, not runny or stiff. If the grits get too thick toward the end of the cooking time, stir in a hot little water. Serve hot.

■ ■ ■

Salmon Croquettes

MAKES 6 SERVINGS

Croquettes for breakfast? They're a favorite of the breakfast crowd at Sylvia's. These croquettes can be made entirely ahead of time and panfried at the last minute. Serve them with fried eggs and grits and pass a basket of warm biscuits.

1 15½-ounce can pink salmon	2 large eggs
1 medium onion, diced	½ cup flour
1 medium green bell pepper, cored, seeded, and diced	1 teaspoon salt
	¼ teaspoon freshly ground black pepper
	Vegetable oil for cooking

1. Drain the can of salmon and place the salmon in a large mixing bowl. Add the remaining ingredients and mix thoroughly. The croquette mixture should be moist and not too chunky.

2. Grease one or two large heavy skillets lightly with oil and heat over medium heat. (A seasoned cast-iron skillet is perfect.) Use about ¼ cup of the croquette mixture to form patties 3 inches across and about ½ inch thick. Cook the croquettes, turning them once, until golden brown on both sides, about 4 minutes. Serve hot.

Note: You may have to cook the croquettes in batches. Keep the cooked ones hot on a baking sheet in a preheated 250°F oven while cooking the rest.

■ ■ ■

Pork

Smothered Pork Chops

MAKES 8 SERVINGS

You'll need two heavy skillets with lids or a large Dutch oven to finish cooking these chops, but it's easier to brown them and make the gravy in one skillet.

8 ¾-inch-thick shoulder pork chops (about 4 pounds)
1 teaspoon plus 1 tablespoon salt
1 teaspoon plus 1 tablespoon freshly ground black pepper
2 cups plus 2 tablespoons all-purpose flour
½ cup vegetable oil

2 large onions, coarsely chopped
2 green bell peppers, cored, seeded, and coarsely chopped
2 stalks celery, coarsely chopped
2 cups water

1. Trim the excess fat from the edges of the pork chops. Sprinkle them with 1 teaspoon each of the salt and pepper. Season 2 cups of the flour with the remaining 1 tablespoon each of salt and pepper. Dredge the pork chops in the flour until coated on all sides. Shake off any excess flour.

2. Pour the vegetable oil into a heavy deep skillet (cast-iron is perfect) over medium-high heat. When the oil begins to shake slightly, add as many pork chops as will fit in the pan without touching. Fry, turning once, until well browned on both sides, about 5 minutes. Remove the chops to a plate and repeat with the remaining chops.

3. Pour off all but 4 tablespoons of drippings from the skillet. Reduce the heat to medium and add the onions, green peppers, and celery to the skillet. Cook until brown and tender, about 10 minutes. Move the vegetables to one side of the skillet and sprinkle the 2 tablespoons of flour over the bottom of the skillet. Cook the

10

flour until golden brown, stirring constantly and being careful not to let the flour burn. Slowly pour in the water and stir until you have a smooth gravy.

4. Divide the pork chops between two heavy skillets with lids or place them all in a large heavy Dutch oven. Top with the gravy and vegetables and cover the skillets or Dutch oven tightly. Simmer over low heat until the vegetables are tender and the pork chops are cooked through, about 15 minutes. Check the seasoning and add salt and pepper as necessary. Serve the pork chops, spooning some of the gravy and vegetables over each. Pass extra gravy.

■ ■ ■

Fried Pork Chops

MAKES 8 SERVINGS

8 ¾-inch-thick shoulder pork
   chops (about 4 pounds)
Salt
Freshly ground black
   pepper

2 cups all-purpose flour
Vegetable oil
Paprika

1. Trim the excess fat from the edges of the pork chops. Sprinkle them generously with salt and pepper.

2. Season the flour generously with salt and pepper. Dredge the pork chops in the flour until coated on all sides. Shake off any excess flour. Pour enough vegetable oil into a heavy deep skillet (cast-iron is perfect) to fill it to 1 inch. Heat over medium heat to 375°F. (A small cube of bread dropped in the oil will brown in about 30 seconds.)

3. Add only as many of the pork chops to the skillet as will fit without touching. Cook them, turning them once, until cooked through (no trace of pink remaining in the center) and deep golden brown, about 12 minutes. Use a long-handled fork or tongs to prevent getting splattered.

4. Remove the pork chops from the skillet to drain. Sprinkle them with paprika and serve hot.

Note: If you like, use two skillets to fry all the pork chops at the same time. If not, keep the first batch of cooked pork chops warm on a baking sheet in a 250°F oven while frying the second batch.

■ ■ ■

Glazed Smoked Ham

MAKES 8 SERVINGS, WITH PLENTY OF LEFTOVERS

A plump, pink smoked ham is a simple and festive centerpiece for any get-together. Leftovers make great eating too, in sandwiches or warmed with a little Brown Gravy (page 29).

1 fully cooked smoked bone-in ham (about 11 pounds)
Granulated sugar

Yellow food coloring (optional)

1. Preheat the oven to 325°F. With a sharp knife, trim all the skin and all but a thin layer of fat from the ham. (Save the skin and fat for dishes like Black-eyed Peas, page 83.) With the tip of the knife, cut a very light diamond pattern into all surfaces of the ham. Rub a light coating of sugar into the ham. If you like, brush the ham lightly with the food coloring.
2. Bake the ham on a rack in a roasting pan until well browned and warmed through, 45 to 60 minutes. Let the ham rest 5 to 10 minutes before carving.
3. Carve the ham into thin slices with a thin slicing knife. Remove any leftover meat from the bone before storing. Save the bone and any trimming for soups and vegetables.

■ ■ ■

Baked Glazed Ham with Pineapple

MAKES 8 SERVINGS, WITH PLENTY OF LEFTOVERS

1 4- to 5-pound cooked smoked boneless ham

1 quart pineapple juice Whole cloves

2 tablespoons plus ½ cup light brown sugar

1 teaspoon ground cinnamon

3 to 4 drops yellow food coloring

1 tablespoon cornstarch

1 8-ounce can sliced pineapple

1. Place the ham in a large bowl or Dutch oven and pour in the pineapple juice. Cover and refrigerate the ham, turning occasionally, overnight.

2. Remove the ham from the liquid and place it fat-side up on a rack in a roasting pan. Reserve 1 cup of the pineapple juice. Score the top of the ham in a diamond pattern, with lines about 1 inch apart. Insert a whole clove into the center of each diamond. Let the ham come to room temperature.

3. Heat the oven to 350°F. Stir 2 tablespoons of the brown sugar and the cinnamon together in a small bowl. Sprinkle this mixture over the ham. Bake the ham 1 hour.

4. To make the pineapple glaze; stir the reserved 1 cup of pineapple liquid, the ½ cup of brown sugar, yellow food coloring, and cornstarch together in a 2-quart saucepan until the cornstarch is dissolved. Heat to simmering over medium heat, stirring constantly, and simmer until the glaze is thickened.

5. Arrange the pineapple slices over the ham, securing them in place with more cloves if necessary, and brush the ham with the pineapple glaze. Continue baking until heated through, about 20 more minutes. Baste several times with the pineapple glaze during this final baking. Remove the ham to a carving board and let stand 10 minutes. Carve into thin slices and serve hot.

Ham Salad

MAKES 8 SERVINGS

Either leftover Glazed Ham (page 13 or page 14) is ideal for making this salad which travels well to picnics or in lunch boxes.

2 cups Hellmann's mayonnaise
1 cup sweet pickle relish
2 teaspoons salt
½ teaspoon freshly ground black pepper
2 pounds cooked smoked boneless ham, finely diced (about 6 cups)

1 medium onion, finely diced (about ½ cup)
1 small green bell pepper, cored, seeded, and finely diced (about 1 cup)
2 stalks celery, finely diced (about 1 cup)

Stir the mayonnaise, relish, salt, and pepper in a large mixing bowl until blended. Add the remaining ingredients and toss until coated. Store the salad, covered, in the refrigerator.

■ ■ ■

Backbone in Gravy

MAKES 8 SERVINGS

Like Barbecued Pigs' Feet (page 64), backbone is a dig-in kind of meal, and the sweet, meaty flavor is worth every bit of effort.

4 pounds fresh meaty pork
  backbone OR pork neck
8 cups plus 1 cup water
3 stalks celery, finely diced
3 green bell peppers, cored,
  seeded, and finely diced

1 onion, finely diced
2 tablespoons salt
1½ tablespoons freshly
  ground black pepper
⅔ cup all-purpose flour

1. Put the backbone and 8 cups of water in a large pot or Dutch oven. Stir in the celery, green peppers, onions, salt, and pepper. Heat over medium heat to boiling. Reduce the heat to simmering and cook, covered, until the meat is tender, about 1½ hours.

2. Stir the flour and 1 cup of water in a small bowl until very smooth. Pour the flour mixture into the cooking liquid and stir constantly until the gravy is simmering and thickened. Simmer 5 minutes and check the seasonings before serving.

■ ■ ■

Pigs' Tails

MAKES 6 SERVINGS

Crunchy, rich pigs' tails are a soul food treat. It's not always easy to find them, but perhaps your butcher can set some aside for you.

2 pounds fresh pigs' tails	2 teaspoons salt
4 cups plus ⅓ cup water	1½ teaspoons crushed red
¼ cup white vinegar	pepper flakes
1 large onion, coarsely chopped	1 teaspoon freshly ground black pepper
1 large stalk celery, coarsely chopped	⅓ cup all-purpose flour

1. Cut each pig tail into 3 pieces. Place them in a 3- to 4-quart saucepan or pot. Add 4 cups of water, the vinegar, onions, celery, salt, red pepper, and black pepper. Bring to a boil over medium heat. Reduce the heat to a simmer and cook, covered, until the tails are tender, about 45 minutes. Occasionally skim the foam that rises to the surface during cooking.
2. Preheat the oven to 350°F. Remove the tails from the broth with a slotted spoon and place them in a shallow baking pan. Reserve the broth. Bake them, turning them occasionally, until nicely browned on all sides, about 30 minutes. Remove and set aside.
3. Meanwhile in a small bowl, stir the flour and ⅓ cup of water until smooth. Stir the flour paste into the reserved cooking liquid. Heat to boiling over medium heat, stirring constantly. Add the pigs' tails to the gravy and simmer 10 to 15 minutes over low heat. Check the seasonings.

■ ■ ■

Fried Chitlins

MAKES 8 SERVINGS

Chitlins are pork small intestines, and like most innards are rich in flavor. In this recipe, chitlins are thoroughly cooked to make them tender before they are quickly fried. Potato Salad (page 81) and Collard Greens (page 98) are the perfect accompaniments. See the note following the recipe for information on buying and preparing chitlins.

3½ **pounds pork chitlins**
4 **cups water**
2 **onions, coarsely chopped**
2 **green bell peppers, cored, seeded, and coarsely chopped**
3 **stalks celery, coarsely chopped**

3 **tablespoons salt**
1 **tablespoon freshly ground black pepper**
1 **tablespoon crushed red pepper flakes**
1½ **cups all-purpose flour**
½ **cup solid vegetable shortening**

1. Place the chitlins in a large saucepan or Dutch oven. Add water, onions, green peppers, celery, 1 tablespoon of the salt, and 1½ teaspoons each of the black pepper and red pepper. Bring to a boil over medium heat, reduce the heat to simmering, and cook, covered, 1 hour.

2. Drain the chitlins well and cool. Cut them into 1- to 1½-inch pieces. Combine the flour with the remaining salt, black pepper, and red pepper. Add the chitlin pieces to the flour a few at a time and toss with a fork to coat on all sides. Remove them to a wire rack or large plate and repeat until all are coated.

3. Heat the shortening in a large heavy skillet over medium heat until a piece of floured chitlin dipped in it gives off a lively sizzle. Carefully add half the chitlins to the skillet. Fry them, turning as necessary, until brown on all sides, about 5 minutes. Remove them with a slotted spoon to paper towels to drain. Repeat with the remaining chitlins. Serve hot.

Note: Precooked chitlins are the most readily available, both fresh and frozen. (Parks ''Famous Flavor'' is a good brand to look for.) If you're using frozen chitlins, defrost them in the container in the warmest part of the refrigerator for 1 to 2 days before cleaning. Precooked chitlins still need to be thoroughly rinsed and drained. For both precooked and uncooked: Wash the chitlins very thoroughly in several changes of cold water, letting them soak a few minutes in each new batch of water. Drain them thoroughly and then cut away any dark spots and fat.

■ ■ ■

Chitlins and Maw

MAKES 8 SERVINGS, WITH PLENTY OF LEFTOVERS

Pork maw is to the pig what tripe is to the cow—that part of the stomach that is prepared for food. It is sometimes available in supermarkets in 1-pound containers. Otherwise, order some from your butcher. Chitlins and maw are great served with Collard Greens (page 98) and Potato Salad (page 81). Ruth and I suggest that if you're going to the trouble of making chitlins, you may as well make a big batch. Leftovers keep well in the refrigerator and are great reheated.

2 pounds pork maw
2 tablespoons salt
2 teaspoons crushed red
   pepper flakes
4 stalks celery, finely chopped
4 small onions, finely
   chopped

4 small green bell peppers,
   cored, seeded, and finely
   chopped
5 pounds precooked
   chitlins

1. Wash the pork maw thoroughly in several changes of cold water. Drain thoroughly and place in a large pot with enough cold water to cover by 2 inches. Add the salt, red pepper, and half of the celery, onions, and green peppers. Heat to boiling, reduce to simmering, and cook, covered, until tender. This could take anywhere from 1½ to 3 hours, depending on the maw.
2. Meanwhile, wash the chitlins carefully in several changes of cold water. Drain thoroughly. Refrigerate until needed.
3. Drain the cooked maw and reserve the cooking liquid. Place the chitlins in a large pot and add enough of the maw cooking liquid to cover by 2 inches. Add the remaining celery, onions, and green peppers. Heat to boiling, reduce to simmering, and cook, covered, until tender, about 1 hour and 30 minutes.

4. Meanwhile, when the pork maw is cool enough to handle, cut it into 1-inch pieces.

5. When the chitlins are tender, stir in the maw pieces and simmer together a few minutes. Check the seasoning and serve hot.

■ ■ ■

Pork Liver Pudding

MAKES 12 SERVINGS

Pork liver pudding is like a soul food pâté. Serve the pudding chilled with crackers as an hors d'oeuvre or at picnics. Pork liver pudding also makes great sandwiches.

1½ pounds fresh pork liver
1 pound fresh pork kidney, cleaned and trimmed of fat and membrane
4 cups water
2 large onions, coarsely chopped
2 stalks celery, coarsely chopped
1 tablespoon crushed red pepper flakes
2 teaspoons salt
1 teaspoon freshly ground black pepper
1 cup cooked rice
1 tablespoon cornstarch
1 medium onion, finely chopped

1. Wash the liver and kidney well. Drain them well on paper towels. Combine the water, liver, kidney, coarsely chopped onions, celery, red pepper, salt, and black pepper in a 5-quart pot. Bring to boil over medium heat. Reduce to a gentle boil, cover, and cook, stirring occasionally, for 1½ hours. Remove the liver and kidney from the pot with a slotted spoon and let stand until cool enough to handle.
2. Pass the liver and kidney and rice through a food mill fitted with the medium disk into a bowl. Sprinkle the cornstarch over the mixture, add the finely chopped onions, and stir until both are incorporated.
3. Pack the mixture into a lightly greased 2½-quart casserole. Cover loosely with plastic wrap and refrigerate 24 hours before serving.

Note: If you don't have a food mill, you can make the pudding by grating the cooked liver and kidney on the largest holes of a 4-sided grater, then puréeing in a food processor.

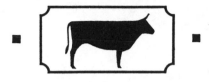

Beef

Ruth's Pot Roast

MAKES 8 SERVINGS

Ruth Gully, our cook at Sylvia's, and I both make great pot roast. We couldn't choose between them, so we decided to include both recipes. You decide which is your favorite.

1 boneless beef rump roast, rolled and tied (about 5 pounds)
2 teaspoons dried thyme
1½ tablespoons salt
1 teaspoon freshly ground black pepper
2 onions, coarsely chopped
2 stalks celery, coarsely chopped

1 large green bell pepper, cored, seeded, and coarsely chopped
⅓ cup all-purpose flour, plus more to coat the roast
3 tablespoons unsalted butter OR margarine
5 cups plus ⅓ cup water

1. Rub the rump roast with the thyme, salt, and black pepper on all sides. Place it in a roasting pan and sprinkle the onions, celery, and green pepper around it. Cover the pan and keep the seasoned roast in the refrigerator several hours or overnight, turning it several times.

2. Preheat the oven to 350°F. Remove the roast from the refrigerator and pat it dry with paper towels. Rub all the sides of the roast with flour. Heat the butter over medium heat in a heavy casserole large enough to fit the roast. Brown the meat well on all sides, turning as necessary. Add the vegetables and 5 cups of water. Cover the casserole and braise in the oven until tender, about 2½ hours. Skim the fat from the cooking liquid and baste the pot roast several times during cooking.

3. Remove the pot roast and let it stand on a platter. Transfer the cooking liquid to a 2-quart saucepan, skim the fat from the surface, and heat to simmering. Stir the ⅓ cup of flour and the ⅓ cup of water together in a small bowl until smooth. Stir the flour mixture into the cooking liquid and simmer, stirring occasionally, until smooth. Adjust the seasonings and simmer 5 minutes. Slice the pot roast into thin slices and serve with the gravy.

■ ■ ■

Sylvia's Pot Roast

MAKES 8 SERVINGS

1 boneless beef rump roast, rolled and tied (about 5 pounds)
2 teaspoons dried thyme
1½ tablespoons salt
1 teaspoon freshly ground black pepper
2 onions, coarsely chopped
2 stalks celery, coarsely chopped
1 large green bell pepper, cored, seeded, and coarsely chopped

⅓ cup all-purpose flour, plus more to coat the roast
3 tablespoons unsalted butter OR margarine
5 cups plus ⅓ cup water
¼ cup A.1. steak sauce
2 tablespoons Worcestershire sauce

1. Rub the rump roast with the thyme, salt, and black pepper on all sides. Place it in a roasting pan and sprinkle the onions, celery, and green peppers around it. Cover the pan and keep the seasoned roast in the refrigerator several hours or overnight, turning it several times.

2. Preheat the oven to 350°F. Remove the roast from the refrigerator and pat it dry with paper towels. Rub all the sides of the roast with flour. Heat the butter over medium heat in a heavy casserole large enough to fit the roast. Brown the meat well on all sides, turning as necessary. Add the vegetables and 5 cups of water. Add the steak sauce and the Worcestershire sauce. Cover the casserole and braise in the oven until tender, about 2½ hours. Skim the fat from the cooking liquid and baste the pot roast several times during cooking.

3. Remove the pot roast and let it stand on a platter. Transfer the cooking liquid to a 2-quart saucepan, skim the fat from the surface, and heat to simmering. Stir the ⅓ cup of flour and the ⅓ cup of water together in a small bowl until smooth. Stir the flour mixture into the cooking liquid and simmer, stirring occasionally, until smooth. Adjust the seasonings and simmer 5 minutes. Slice the pot roast into thin slices and serve with the gravy.

■ ■ ■

Short Ribs in Gravy

MAKES 8 SERVINGS

4 pounds beef short ribs, sliced across the bone 1 inch thick

8 cups plus 1½ cups water

2 large onions, coarsely chopped

3 green bell peppers, cored, seeded, and coarsely chopped

4 stalks celery, coarsely chopped

1 tablespoon plus 1 teaspoon salt

1 tablespoon freshly ground black pepper

¾ cup all-purpose flour

1. Wash the short ribs and pat them dry with paper towels. Place the short ribs, 8 cups of water, onions, green peppers, celery, salt, and pepper in a heavy 6-quart pot. Heat over medium-high heat until boiling. Reduce the heat to simmering and simmer until the short ribs are tender, about 1½ to 2 hours. Remove the short ribs to a bowl and keep warm.

2. Place the flour in a bowl and beat in 1½ cups of water to make a smooth thin paste. Slowly pour this mixture into the cooking liquid, stirring constantly. Return the short ribs to the pot. Check the seasoning and add salt and pepper if necessary. Simmer 10 minutes and serve hot.

Note: The short ribs can be prepared entirely ahead up to 3 or 4 days before serving. Let them stand at room temperature for 1 hour before heating. Heat the short ribs in a large heavy pot over low heat, stirring often, until they are heated through. Check the thickness and seasoning of the gravy. You might have to add a little water to thin it or some salt and pepper.

■ ■ ■

Brown Gravy

MAKES ABOUT 5 CUPS

Short ribs give this gravy a rich, meaty flavor and make a bonus meal too. It's great on grits and mashed potatoes.

3 pounds beef short ribs
2 teaspoons salt
½ teaspoon freshly ground black pepper
⅔ cup all-purpose flour
1⅓ cups water

1 tablespoon GravyMaster
2 medium onions, thinly sliced
2 green bell peppers, cored, seeded, and thinly sliced

1. Rinse the short ribs under cold running water and drain them thoroughly. Place them in a heavy 5-quart pot. Add enough cold water to cover the ribs (about 8 cups) and add the salt and pepper. Heat over high heat to boiling. Reduce the heat and simmer until the ribs are tender, about 2½ hours. Skim the surface of the liquid occasionally during cooking.
2. Remove the ribs and save them for another use (Barbecued Short Ribs, page 61).
3. Stir the flour into the water until smooth. Stir in the Gravy-Master. Slowly mix the flour mixture into the short rib liquid, stirring constantly. Simmer until smooth and thickened. Check the seasonings, stir in the sliced onions and green peppers, and simmer 10 minutes.

■ ■ ■

Roast Beef and Gravy

MAKES 8 SERVINGS, WITH LEFTOVERS

1 4-pound top round roast	GRAVY
2 stalks celery, finely chopped	
2 onions, finely chopped	¼ cup all-purpose flour
2 green bell peppers, cored, seeded, and finely chopped	½ cup water
	1 teaspoon GravyMaster
1 tablespoon salt	2 onions, thinly sliced
2 teaspoons freshly ground black pepper	1 green bell pepper, cored, seeded, and thinly sliced
	Salt and freshly ground black pepper to taste

1. Wash the top round and pat it dry with paper towels. Rub it with the chopped celery, onions, and green peppers and salt and pepper on all sides.

2. Preheat the oven to 400°F. Place the beef in a roasting pan and pour in enough water to fill the pan to 1 inch. Roast 15 minutes. Reduce heat to 350°F and continue roasting until a meat thermometer inserted into the thickest part of the roast reads 130°F.

3. Remove the beef from the roasting pan and strain the cooking liquid into a small saucepan. (There should be about 2 cups; if not, add water as necessary.) Return the beef to the roasting pan and continue roasting until the outside is brown and the thermometer reads 140°F for medium-rare, about 10 minutes.

4. Meanwhile, make the gravy: Stir the flour and water together until smooth. Heat the cooking liquid over low heat to simmering.

Stir in enough of the flour mixture to make a gravy thick enough to coat a spoon. Add the GravyMaster. Add the sliced onions and green peppers and season with salt and pepper. Simmer 10 minutes.

5. Remove the roast and let it stand 10 minutes. Slice it thin and serve warm with gravy.

■ ■ ■

Smothered Steak

MAKES 6 SERVINGS

1 piece of round steak, 1 inch thick (about 2¼ pounds)

1 tablespoon plus 1 teaspoon salt

1 tablespoon plus 1 teaspoon freshly ground black pepper

2 cups plus 2 tablespoons all-purpose flour

¼ cup vegetable oil

2 large onions, coarsely chopped

2 green bell peppers, cored, seeded, and coarsely chopped

2 stalks celery, coarsely chopped

1 cup water

1. Wash the steak and pat it dry with paper towels. Rub 1 tablespoon each of the salt and pepper into all sides of the steak. Combine 2 cups of the flour and the remaining 1 teaspoon each of salt and pepper on a large plate and stir to mix. Dredge the steak in the seasoned flour until well coated. Shake off any excess flour.

2. Pour the vegetable oil in a heavy skillet large enough to hold the steak comfortably. Heat over medium-high heat until the oil begins to shake slightly. Add the steak and fry, turning as necessary, until well browned on all sides, about 5 minutes. Remove it to a plate.

3. Pour off all but 2 tablespoons of drippings from the skillet. Reduce the heat to medium and add the onions, green peppers, and celery to skillet. Cook until tender, stirring occasionally. Move the vegetables to one side of the skillet and add the 2 tablespoons of flour to the other side. Cook, stirring, until the flour is golden, about 6 minutes. Slowly pour in the water and stir until the gravy is smooth.

4. Return the steak to the skillet and cook, turning once, 15 minutes for a medium steak, or longer for a more well done and more tender steak.

5. Remove the steak to a serving platter. Check the sauce—if it's too thick, add a little water. Adjust the seasonings. Slice the steak and serve with the gravy.

■ ■ ■

Meat Loaf

MAKES 10 SERVINGS

Ruth has made so many of these over the years she can tell when the meat loaf is finished baking just by looking at it. "There should be cracks in the top and the juices are kind of yellow, not pink. And if you are lucky enough to have some leftover biscuits, use them instead of bread."

Cold meat loaf makes great sandwiches or try this quick method for using leftovers: Cut the meat loaf into 1-inch cubes and fry them in a little oil over medium heat until they're heated through and browned.

2 **cups day-old bread (Biscuits, page 2, are perfect, otherwise, use good-quality white bread)**
¾ **cup milk**
3 **pounds lean ground beef**
2 **stalks celery, chopped**
1 **green bell pepper, cored, seeded, and chopped**
2 **small onions, chopped**
2½ **teaspoons poultry seasoning**
1 **tablespoon salt**
1 **teaspoon crushed red pepper flakes**
¾ **cup plus 3 tablespoons tomato purée**
5 **large eggs**

1. Preheat the oven to 350°F. Place a pan of water on the lowest rack. Set the other rack in the center of the oven.
2. Crumble the bread into a large bowl. Pour in the milk and let stand, mixing once or twice, until the bread has soaked up the milk.
3. Add all the remaining ingredients to the soaked bread except the 3 tablespoons of tomato purée. Mix well with your hands, making sure there are no lumps of unmixed bread or meat.
4. Place the meat on a deep baking sheet and pat it with your hands into a loaf shape about 6 inches thick. Smooth the outside. Spread the 3 tablespoons of tomato purée over the outside of the loaf. Bake on a rack in the center of the oven until the juices from the center

run clear, not pink, about 1 hour. Drain or spoon the fat from the pan occasionally during roasting to prevent the meat loaf from becoming greasy.

5. Let the meat loaf stand about 5 minutes before serving. Slice the meat loaf into 1-inch-thick pieces and serve with Meat Loaf Gravy.

■ ■ ■

Meat Loaf Gravy

MAKES ABOUT 6 CUPS, ENOUGH FOR 12 SERVINGS OF MEAT LOAF

This simple gravy is the perfect thing for our flavorful meat loaf. If there's any left over, it can be served with mashed potatoes.

1 28-ounce can tomato purée
3 cups water
1 small onion, thinly sliced
1 small green bell pepper, cored, seeded, and thinly sliced

1 small stalk celery, thinly sliced
1 teaspoon sugar
2 teaspoons salt
¼ teaspoon freshly ground black pepper

Combine all the ingredients in a heavy pot and heat, stirring occasionally, until very hot, but not boiling. (Boiling will thin the gravy.) Check the seasoning and serve hot over meat loaf.

Note: Leftover meat loaf gravy can be refrigerated for up to 1 week.

■ ■ ■

Oxtails in Gravy

MAKES 6 SERVINGS

Tough cuts of meat, like oxtails, are the best value because they are the least expensive but have the most flavor. Slowly simmering these tough cuts makes for a rich gravy and tender meat. Serve oxtails with Collard Greens (page 98) and Black-eyed Peas (page 83).

3 **pounds oxtails (about 2 tails)**
6 **cups plus 1 cup water**
2 **large onions, coarsely chopped**
2 **green bell peppers, cored, seeded, and coarsely chopped**

2 **stalks celery, coarsely chopped**
1 **tablespoon salt**
2 **teaspoons freshly ground black pepper**
½ **cup all-purpose flour**

1. Wash the oxtails and pat them dry with paper towels. Place the oxtails, 6 cups of water, onions, green peppers, celery, salt, and pepper in a heavy 6-quart pot. Heat over medium-high heat until boiling. Reduce the heat to simmering and simmer until the oxtails are tender, about 2 hours.

2. Place the flour in a bowl and stir in 1 cup of water to make a smooth thin paste. Slowly pour the flour paste into the cooking liquid, stirring constantly. Check the seasoning and add salt and pepper if necessary. Simmer 10 minutes and serve hot.

Note: The oxtails can be prepared entirely ahead up to 3 or 4 days before serving. Let them stand at room temperature for 1 hour before heating. Heat the oxtails in a large heavy pot over low heat, stirring often, until they are heated through. Check the thickness and seasoning of the gravy. You might have to add a little water to thin it or some salt and pepper.

Grilled Beef Liver

MAKES 4 SERVINGS

The large griddle at Sylvia's is perfect for cooking thick slices of beef liver and for sautéing onions and peppers to go with them. At home, you can get restaurant-quality results by using a large heavy skillet—cast-iron is ideal.

Vegetable oil
1 large onion, sliced ½ inch thick
1 large green bell pepper, cored, seeded, and sliced ½ inch thick

4 ½-inch slices beef liver (about 6 ounces each)
Salt
Freshly ground black pepper
1 cup all-purpose flour

1. Heat enough vegetable oil to coat the bottom of a large (12-inch) heavy skillet over medium heat. Add the onion and green pepper, sprinkle them with salt and pepper, and cook until tender, about 15 minutes. Remove the vegetables from the skillet.
2. Sprinkle the slices of liver with salt and pepper and dredge them in flour. Add ¼ inch of vegetable oil to the skillet and heat over medium-high heat until a little flour sprinkled into the oil gives off a lively sizzle. Fry the liver slices, turning them once, until cooked through, about 8 minutes, and drain them on paper towels. Pour off any oil from the skillet. Return the vegetables to the skillet and heat them until warmed through. Serve with the liver slices.

Note Chicken livers can be "grilled" in the same way. Substitute about 1¼ pounds chicken livers, trimmed of fat and gristle, for the beef liver.

■ ■ ■

Poultry

Fried Chicken

MAKES 8 SERVINGS

Crispy-skinned fried chicken, hot from the pan and bursting with juice, is one of the simplest and best-tasting soul food classics and one of our most popular dishes at Sylvia's. Serve the chicken with Giblet Gravy (page 49) and any or all of the following "sides": Black-eyed Peas (page 83), Collard Greens (page 98), Potato Salad (page 81), and Boiled String Beans with Ham (page 95).

2 3½-pound frying chickens, cut into 8 pieces
Salt
Freshly ground black pepper

2 cups all-purpose flour
2 tablespoons paprika, plus more for the finished chicken
Vegetable oil

1. Trim the excess fat and skin from each piece of chicken. Sprinkle the pieces with salt and pepper. Stir the flour and paprika together in a shallow bowl. Dredge the chicken pieces in the seasoned flour to coat on all sides. Shake off the excess flour.

2. Pour enough vegetable oil into a heavy deep skillet (cast-iron is perfect) to fill it to 2 inches. Heat over medium heat to 375°F. (A small cube of bread dropped in the oil will brown in about 20 seconds.)

3. Add only as many of the chicken pieces as will fit without touching. Overcrowding will lower the temperature of the oil and make your fried chicken greasy. With a long-handled fork or tongs to prevent getting splattered, turn the chicken pieces until they are golden brown on all sides and cooked through, about 6 minutes. The easiest way to tell if the chicken is cooked is to poke a fork down to the bone near the thickest part—if the chicken is cooked the juices will run clear, not pink.

4. Remove the chicken pieces from the skillet to drain. If you have to fry the chicken in batches, keep the fried chicken warm on a baking sheet in a 250°F oven. When all the chicken is fried, sprinkle the pieces with paprika and serve hot.

■ ■ ■

Smothered Chicken

MAKES 8 SERVINGS

2 3½-pound frying chickens, each cut into 8 pieces
1 teaspoon plus 1 tablespoon salt
1 teaspoon plus 1 tablespoon freshly ground black pepper
2 cups plus 2 tablespoons all-purpose flour
½ cup vegetable oil

2 large onions, coarsely chopped
2 green bell peppers, cored, seeded, and coarsely chopped
2 stalks celery, coarsely chopped
2 cups water

1. Trim the excess fat from the chicken pieces and sprinkle them with 1 teaspoon each of the salt and pepper. Season 2 cups of the flour with the remaining 1 tablespoon each of salt and pepper. Dredge the chicken pieces in the flour until coated on all sides. Shake off any excess flour.
2. Heat the vegetable oil in a heavy deep skillet (cast-iron is perfect) over medium heat until the edge of a chicken piece dipped into the oil gives off a lively sizzle. Add as many chicken pieces to the skillet as will fit without touching. Fry until the pieces are browned on all sides, about 6 minutes. Adjust the heat as necessary during frying to keep a lively sizzle without overbrowning. Remove the fried chicken to drain and repeat with the remaining pieces.
3. Pour off all but 4 tablespoons of drippings from the skillet. Reduce the heat to medium and add the onions, peppers, and celery to the skillet. Cook, stirring occasionally, until brown and tender, about 10 minutes. Move the vegetables to one side of the skillet and sprinkle the 2 tablespoons of flour over the other side of the skillet. Cook the flour until golden brown, stirring constantly. Be careful not to let the flour burn. Slowly pour in the water and stir until the gravy is smooth.

4. Divide the chicken between two heavy skillets with lids or place them all in a large heavy Dutch oven. Top with the gravy and vegetables and cover the skillets or Dutch oven tightly. Simmer over low heat until the vegetables are tender and the chicken is cooked through, about 15 minutes. Check the seasoning and add salt and pepper as necessary. Serve the chicken, spooning some of the gravy and vegetables over each piece. Pass extra gravy.

■ ■ ■

Chicken Vegetable Soup

MAKES ABOUT 8 QUARTS, ENOUGH FOR 12 GENEROUS SERVINGS

2 2½-pound chickens, each
   cut into 12 pieces
5 quarts water
1 tablespoon poultry
   seasoning
1 tablespoon sugar
1 tablespoon plus 1 teaspoon
   salt
2 teaspoons freshly ground
   black pepper
1 28-ounce can whole
   tomatoes
4 Idaho potatoes, peeled and
   finely diced (about 3 cups)
5 carrots, peeled and finely
   chopped (about 2 cups)
5 stalks celery with leaves,
   trimmed and finely chopped
   (about 2 cups)

¼ small green cabbage,
   finely chopped (about 2
   cups)
2 medium onions, peeled
   and finely chopped
   (about 2 cups)
1 large turnip, peeled and
   finely chopped (about 2
   cups)
2 green bell peppers,
   cored, seeded, and finely
   chopped (about 1½ cups)
1 cup small macaroni, such
   as elbow or ditali

1. Place the chicken pieces in a large (4-gallon) soup pot. Add the water, poultry seasoning, sugar, salt, and pepper. Heat to boiling, reduce the heat to a simmer, and cook 20 minutes. Add the remaining ingredients except the macaroni. Return to a simmer and cook 1 hour and 15 minutes.

2. Add the macaroni and cook 15 more minutes, stirring occasionally. Adjust the seasoning and serve hot.

■ ■ ■

Southern Chicken and Rice Perlow

MAKES 4 SERVINGS

Perlow is the Southern name given to any dish that's cooked with rice, like this chicken or the Fried Chitlins on page 18.

1 3½- to 4-pound chicken, cut into 8 pieces
  Giblets from the chicken
2 quarts water
2 medium onions, finely chopped (about 2 cups)
3 stalks celery, finely chopped (about 2 cups)
1 green bell pepper, finely chopped (about 1½ cups)

2 tablespoons salt
½ teaspoon freshly ground black pepper
½ teaspoon crushed red pepper flakes
½ teaspoon poultry seasoning
4 cups converted rice

1. Combine all the ingredients except the rice in a 5-quart pot. Cover and heat to boiling. Reduce the heat to simmering and cook, covered, 15 minutes, stirring once or twice.
2. Slowly stir in the rice and return to a simmer. Stir well, cover, and simmer until the rice is tender, about 30 minutes. Serve hot.

■ ■ ■

Chicken and Dumplings

MAKES 6 SERVINGS

One-pot meals are great for cold-weather eating. This particular dish is a very simple one to put together—the dumplings are made and rolled while the chicken is simmering. The whole affair from start to end takes about 1 hour.

1 3½-pound chicken, cut into 8 pieces
4 cups water
3 onions, finely chopped
3 stalks celery, finely chopped
3 green bell peppers, cored, seeded, and finely chopped
1 tablespoon salt
1 teaspoon freshly ground black pepper

2½ cups all-purpose flour, plus more for kneading
3 tablespoons sugar
2 teaspoons baking powder
1½ cups milk
3 large eggs, beaten
½ cup solid vegetable shortening

1. Wash the chicken pieces and drain them well. Put them with the water, onions, celery, green peppers, salt, and pepper in a large pot or Dutch oven. Heat over medium heat to boiling. Reduce the heat to simmering and cook 10 minutes.
2. Meanwhile, make the dumplings: Stir the flour, sugar, and baking powder in a large bowl until combined. Make a well in the center and add the milk, eggs, and shortening. Mix the wet ingredients into the dry ingredients with your fingers until they form a smooth, soft dough. Turn the dough onto a lightly floured board.
3. Check the chicken pot—there should be enough cooking liquid to barely cover the chicken and vegetables. If not, add hot water as necessary. Lightly flour your hands and roll the dumpling dough into 1-inch balls. Drop the dumplings into the pot of simmering chicken until they cover the surface in a single layer. Cover the pot

and boil 15 minutes. Reduce the heat and simmer until the dumplings are light and cooked through, about 5 minutes. Serve the chicken and vegetables with some dumplings and liquid.

■ ■ ■

Sweet and Spicy Chicken Wings

MAKES 6 SERVINGS

These delicious wings go great with rice and broccoli, and are even better if you let them marinate in the sauce overnight before baking.

1½ tablespoons salt
 ½ teaspoon freshly ground
    black pepper
 ½ teaspoon garlic powder
 3 pounds chicken wings
 ½ cup sugar

 ½ cup water
 ½ cup lemon juice
 ½ cup orange marmalade
 8 tablespoons (1 stick)
    unsalted butter

1. Mix the salt, pepper, and garlic powder together and rub this spice mixture into the chicken wings. Place the wings in a single layer in an 11- by 7-inch baking pan.
2. Preheat the oven to 400°F. Combine the sugar, water, lemon juice, marmalade, and butter in a small saucepan over medium heat. Stir until the butter is melted. Remove the sauce from the heat and let stand 10 minutes. Pour the sauce over the chicken wings and bake until they are cooked through and golden brown, about 35 minutes.

■ ■ ■

Roast Turkey

MAKES 12 SERVINGS

1 14- to 16-pound turkey
½ cup kosher salt
2 teaspoons garlic powder
1 large onion, diced
1 orange, cut into eighths
3 stalks celery, coarsely
   chopped

8 tablespoons (1 stick)
   unsalted butter OR
   margarine
½ teaspoon salt
½ teaspoon freshly ground
   black pepper
½ teaspoon paprika

1. Remove the giblets and neck from the cavity of the turkey. If you like, use them to prepare Giblet Gravy (page 49) for the turkey.

2. Rinse the turkey inside and out under cold running water. Place the turkey in a pot large enough to hold it comfortably and add enough cold water to cover the turkey. Add the kosher salt and garlic powder to the pot. Soak the turkey for 2 hours.

3. Preheat the oven to 450°F. Remove the turkey, drain well, and pat dry inside and out with paper towels. Place the onions, orange slices, celery, and butter in the cavity. Rub the outside with a mixture of salt, pepper, and paprika. Tighten the skin of the turkey by placing it in the 450°F oven for 15 minutes. Turn the oven down to 350°F. Roast the turkey, basting occasionally, until the juice runs clear when you pierce the thickest part of the thigh (180°F on a meat thermometer, about 3 hours). Remove from the oven and let stand about 20 minutes before carving.

■ ■ ■

Giblet Gravy

MAKES 2 CUPS

3 cups plus 2 tablespoons water
Giblets from turkey
1 medium onion, finely chopped (about 1 cup)
1 green bell pepper, cored, seeded, and finely chopped (about 1 cup)

2 stalks celery, chopped (about 1 cup)
1 teaspoon salt
1 teaspoon freshly ground black pepper
1 teaspoon poultry seasoning
1 tablespoon cornstarch

1. Combine all the ingredients except the 2 tablespoons of the water and the cornstarch in a 4-quart saucepan. Cover, heat to boiling, and reduce to a simmer. Simmer, covered, until the giblet are tender, about 45 minutes.

2. Use a slotted spoon to remove the giblets and cool to room temperature. Do not discard the liquid. Chop them into small pieces. Return the giblet pieces to the saucepan and check the seasoning. Dissolve the cornstarch in 2 tablespoons of water in a small bowl. Stir the cornstarch mixture into the giblet mixture and simmer, stirring, until thickened.

■ ■ ■

Corn Bread Dressing

MAKES 6 SERVINGS

If you're using this dressing to stuff a turkey, use the giblets, neck, and liver from the turkey instead of the chicken parts called for in this recipe. This dressing is perfect with simmered turkey wings (page 52) or with roasted chicken and other birds.

Giblets, necks, and livers from 4 chickens
1 stalk celery, coarsely chopped
1 onion, coarsely chopped
1 green bell pepper, cored, seeded, and coarsely chopped
4 cups day-old corn bread, very finely crumbled
1 stalk celery, finely chopped
1 medium onion, finely chopped

1 green bell pepper, cored, seeded, and finely diced
1 teaspoon crushed red pepper flakes
1 teaspoon salt
Drippings from a roasted turkey OR liquid from cooking turkey wings (page 52)

1. Combine the giblets, necks, and livers and the coarsely chopped celery, onions, and green peppers, in a 3-quart saucepan. Add enough cold water to cover all the ingredients by about 1 inch. Heat to boiling, then reduce the heat to simmer. Remove the livers after about 10 minutes. Remove everything else when the vegetables are tender, about 20 minutes. Discard the vegetables. Chop the giblets and livers very finely and pull the meat from the neck and set aside.

2. Preheat the oven to 350°F. Combine the crumbled corn bread, finely chopped celery, onions, and green peppers, the red pepper, salt, and chopped innards in a large bowl. Mix with your hands while adding enough turkey drippings to make a wet but not soupy dressing. Transfer to an 11- by 7-inch baking dish. Cover with aluminum foil.

3. Bake the dressing until the innards are very tender, about 40 minutes.

■ ■ ■

Turkey Wings and Gravy

MAKES 6 SERVINGS

The tougher cuts of meat and poultry are the least expensive and have the most flavor. Turkey wings, available most everywhere, are a perfect example of this. Simmered gently and served with Corn Bread Dressing (page 50), they make a delicious dinner.

6 turkey wings (about 3¼ pounds)
2 stalks celery, sliced about ½ inch thick
1 small onion, thinly sliced
1 medium green bell pepper, cored, seeded, and thinly sliced
1½ teaspoons poultry seasoning

2 teaspoons salt
¼ teaspoon freshly ground black pepper
¼ cup all-purpose flour
½ cup water
1 to 2 teaspoons GravyMaster

1. Cut each wing into 3 pieces at the joints. Place the wing pieces, celery, onions, and green peppers in a large pot with enough cold water to cover. Add the poultry seasoning, salt, and pepper and heat to boiling. Reduce the heat to simmering and simmer until the wing pieces are very tender, about 1½ hours. Check the seasoning once or twice during cooking and adjust as necessary.

2. In a bowl, stir the flour into the water until smooth. Slowly stir the flour mixture into the simmering turkey liquid until it is smooth and thickened. Stir in the GravyMaster. Taste the gravy and add seasoning if necessary. Thin the gravy with a little water if necessary. Serve hot, passing extra gravy.

Note: The wings can be prepared entirely in advance. To serve, heat over a low flame, adding a little water to thin the gravy if necessary.

Glazed Cornish Hens

MAKES 4 SERVINGS

2 1½-pound Cornish hens
1½ teaspoons salt
1 teaspoon freshly ground
  black pepper
1 teaspoon poultry
  seasoning, if desired
1 small onion, finely
  chopped (about ½ cup)

1 green bell pepper, cored,
  seeded, and finely
  chopped
3 tablespoons unsalted
  butter OR margarine
1 tablespoon honey

1. Preheat the oven to 350°F. Rinse the hens under cold water and pat them dry inside and out with paper towels. Mix the salt, pepper, and poultry seasoning in a small bowl and sprinkle half the mixture inside the hens. Divide the chopped onions and green peppers between the cavities of the 2 hens. Rub the rest of the seasoning mixture into the skin.
2. Combine the butter and honey in a small saucepan over low heat. Stir until the butter is melted and the mixture is smooth. Roast the hens, basting occasionally with the honey mixture, until no trace of pink remains in the thickest part of the thigh and they are well browned, about 1 hour and 15 minutes. Remove and let stand 5 minutes before serving.

■ ■ ■

Cornish Hens with Rice

MAKES 8 SERVINGS

The rice stuffing mixture makes enough to stuff the four birds plus serve as a side dish. If you'd like only enough to stuff the birds, cut the amount of stuffing ingredients in half.

THE BIRDS

- 4 Cornish hens (each about 1¼ pounds), with giblets
- 2 tablespoons salt
- 1 tablespoon freshly ground white pepper
- 8 tablespoons (1 stick) melted unsalted butter OR margarine

THE STUFFING

- 2½ cups water
  Giblets from the Cornish hens
- 2 onions, finely chopped
- 2 green bell peppers, finely chopped
- 2 stalks celery, finely chopped
- 1 tablespoon salt
- 2 teaspoons crushed red pepper flakes
- ¼ cup bacon drippings
- 2 cups rice

1. Preheat the oven to 450°F. Remove the giblets from the hens and set them aside. Rinse the hens and pat them dry inside and out with paper towels. Sprinkle the hens inside and out with salt and pepper and place them breast-side up in a shallow baking dish or roasting pan. Brush the skin with melted butter. Roast the hens 15 minutes and remove to cool. Lower the oven to 350°F.

2. Meanwhile, prepare the rice stuffing. Pour 2½ cups water into a heavy 2-quart saucepan. Add the giblets, onions, green peppers, celery, salt, red pepper, and bacon drippings. Heat to boiling, cover, and cook until the vegetables are tender, about 10 minutes.

Add the rice and reduce the heat to very low and cook, covered, until the rice is tender, about 20 minutes. Remove the giblets and chop them finely and return them to the rice.

3. Spoon the hot rice into the birds. Don't pack the stuffing too tightly—it will expand a little during cooking. Return the hens to the oven and roast until the juice runs clear when you pierce the thickest part of the thigh and the hens are deep golden brown, about 35 minutes. Brush once or twice more with the melted butter. Spoon the rice from the hens into a serving bowl, cut the hens into 4 pieces each, and serve.

■ ■ ■

Wild Rice Stuffing

MAKES ABOUT 5 CUPS

This is perfect stuffing for Glazed Cornish Hens (page 53) or a large roaster chicken. Any leftover stuffing can be heated in a covered baking dish and served with the birds.

½ **pound skinless breakfast sausage OR one quarter recipe Pork Breakfast Sausages (page 5)**

1 **medium green bell pepper, cored, seeded, and finely diced (about ½ cup)**

1 **medium onion, finely diced (about ½ cup)**

1 **teaspoon salt**

½ **teaspoon freshly ground black pepper**

½ **teaspoon tarragon**

1 **pound wild rice, cooked and drained (about 5 cups)**

Crumble the sausage into a large heavy skillet. Cook over medium heat until the sausage renders its fat and begins to brown. Add the green peppers and onions and continue cooking until they are tender and the sausage is brown and no trace of pink remains, about 10 minutes. Season with the salt, pepper, and tarragon. Toss well with the wild rice. Let the stuffing stand a few minutes and adjust the seasonings.

■ ■ ■

Barbecue

Sylvia's World-Famous Talked-About Spareribs

MAKES 8 SERVINGS

These are the real thing. People come from around the corner, around the city, and around the world to eat these ribs at Sylvia's. The secret? Tangy, not too sweet barbecue sauce and a special way of preparing the ribs that's described here.

2 slabs pork spareribs
(about 3½ pounds total)
1½ teaspoons salt
½ teaspoon freshly ground
black pepper

½ teaspoon crushed red
pepper flakes
2 to 3 cups white wine
vinegar
Barbecue Sauce (page 59)

1. To make the ribs easier to handle, cut each slab between the middle bones into 2 equal pieces. Rub the salt, black pepper, and red pepper into both sides of the ribs. Place the ribs in a deep baking dish, cover them, and refrigerate overnight.

2. Preheat the oven to 450°F. Pour the vinegar over the ribs and bake 1½ hours. Rotate the ribs two or three times during baking and spoon some of the pan juices over them.

3. Remove the ribs from the baking dish and place in a single layer on baking sheets. (Line the baking sheets with aluminum foil for easy cleanup.) Bake at 450°F for 1 hour. The ribs should be tender and well browned. This much can be done up to a day in advance. Cool the ribs, cover tightly, and refrigerate. Bring to room temperature for about 1 hour before continuing.

4. To finish the ribs, preheat the oven to 400°F. Cut the slabs between the bones into individual ribs. Place the ribs in a baking dish large enough to hold them comfortably. Spoon enough of the barbecue sauce over them to coat lightly. Cover the pan with aluminum foil and bake until heated through, about 20 minutes. Serve with additional barbecue sauce on the side.

■ ■ ■

Barbecue Sauce

MAKES ABOUT 5 CUPS

Ruth developed this recipe because she found most barbecue sauces too vinegary or bitter, and it's the secret to our popular ribs. Simple to prepare and absolutely delicious, once made and strained it keeps for quite a while, at least a month—that is, if you can keep from using it that long.

16 ounces Red Devil Hot Sauce	3 cups tomato purée
2½ teaspoons crushed red pepper flakes	1½ cups water
1 small onion, sliced	1½ cups sugar
1 small stalk celery, sliced	1 lemon, sliced

Combine all the ingredients in a heavy pot and heat just till hot. Don't bring to a boil or the sauce will turn dark and become thin. Cool the sauce to room temperature, strain it, and store it in a tightly covered jar in the refrigerator.

■ ■ ■

Southern Spareribs

MAKES 6 SERVINGS

Pork ribs prepared in this manner cook slowly in the sauce and are mellower than the tangy Barbecued Short Ribs of Beef on page 61. These are great for parties as they can be prepared completely in advance.

6 pounds pork ribs, in 2
   pieces
1 teaspoon salt
1 teaspoon freshly ground
   black pepper
1 6-ounce can tomato juice
1 medium onion, finely
   chopped (about ½ cup)

½ cup cider vinegar
½ cup firmly packed dark
   brown sugar
¼ cup vegetable oil
 1 tablespoon
   Worcestershire sauce
1 teaspoon dry mustard

1. Season the ribs with salt and pepper and place them in a 17- by 12- by 12-inch disposable aluminum foil roasting pan. Combine the remaining ingredients in a bowl and stir until thoroughly blended. Pour the marinade over the ribs, making sure the marinade coats all sides of them. Cover and refrigerate 3 hours to overnight.
2. Preheat the oven to 350°F. Cover the roasting pan with heavy-duty aluminum foil and bake until the ribs are tender, about 1 hour. Cut the ribs into 2- to 3-rib sections before serving and, if you like, skim some of the fat from the sauce before passing it around with the ribs.

■ ■ ■

Barbecued Short Ribs of Beef

MAKES 6 SERVINGS

Short ribs prepared this way are rich and meaty. For even more flavor, marinate the ribs overnight before cooking. You may use any barbecue sauce you like to baste the ribs during the final cooking, but of course we're partial to Sylvia's own sauce.

3 to 4 **pounds short ribs of beef, cut across the bone 1 to 1½ inches thick**
2 **teaspoons salt**
1 **teaspoon freshly ground black pepper**

1 **cup cider vinegar**
1 **cup soy sauce**
2 **quarts water**
Barbecue Sauce (page 59)

1. Season the ribs with salt and pepper. Put them into a large bowl and add the vinegar and soy sauce. Marinate at room temperature 1 to 2 hours, or covered in the refrigerator overnight, turning the ribs occasionally.
2. Preheat the oven to 350°F. Remove the ribs from the marinade and place in an 18- by 12-inch roasting pan. Pour in the water and bake, covered, until tender, about 1½ hours.
3. Pour off and discard the cooking liquid. Baste the ribs well with barbecue sauce. Return the pan to the oven and bake, basting with barbecue sauce once or twice, until well browned, about 30 minutes. Serve hot, passing extra sauce separately.

■ ■ ■

Chopped Barbecue

MAKES 8 SERVINGS

Chopped Barbecue, which mixes the crusty outer part of the pork with the juicy center part and is seasoned with onions and peppers, makes a great sandwich. Serve with Potato Salad (page 81) and Coleslaw (page 105).

3 pounds bone-in pork shoulder roast OR 2½ pounds pork roast, boned and rolled
2 tablespoons crushed red pepper flakes
2 teaspoons salt
1 teaspoon freshly ground black pepper

½ to 1 cup white vinegar
2 medium onions, finely chopped (about 1½ cups)
1 green bell pepper, cored, seeded, and chopped (about ½ cup)
2 cups Barbecue Sauce (page 59)

1. Rinse the pork roast and pat it dry with paper towels. Combine the red pepper, salt, and black pepper. Rub the mixture into all sides of the pork. Cover loosely with waxed paper and refrigerate overnight.

2. Place the seasoned pork in a shallow roasting pan and let stand at room temperature 1 hour.

3. Preheat the oven to 300°F. Pour the vinegar to taste over the pork (more for a sharper flavor, less for a more mellow flavor). Scatter the chopped onions and green peppers into the pan. Roast the meat until a thermometer inserted into the thickest part of the roast registers 180°F. Spoon the pan juices over the pork a few times during roasting. Remove the roast and let stand 1 hour. Keep the pan juices.

4. Remove the meat from the bone, if necessary, and chop it into roughly ¼-inch pieces. Heat the barbecue sauce in a large saucepan over low heat until hot. Skim the fat from the pan drippings and add the drippings to the barbecue sauce. Stir the pork, onions and green peppers into the sauce and warm without boiling until heated through. Serve hot.

Note: To serve a barbecued pork shoulder, simply prepare this recipe through Step 3 and serve the pork whole, sliced thin.

■ ■ ■

Barbecued Pigs' Feet

MAKES 8 SERVINGS

Pigs' feet are short on meat but long on flavor—and they're fun to eat. Tuck a napkin into your shirt, grab a stack for the table, and get into the spirit.

8 fresh pigs' feet (about 5 pounds), split in half lengthwise
2 quarts water
2 cups white vinegar
2 large onions, coarsely chopped
2 green bell peppers, cored, seeded, and coarsely chopped

¼ cup crushed red pepper flakes
3 tablespoons salt
1 tablespoon freshly ground black pepper
3 cups Barbecue Sauce (page 59), at room temperature

1. Wash the pigs' feet well. Place them in a large pot and pour in the water. Add the vinegar, onions, green peppers, red pepper, salt, and black pepper. Heat to boiling over medium heat. Reduce the heat to simmering and cook, covered, until just about tender, about 2½ hours. Skim the surface and stir the pigs' feet occasionally during cooking.
2. Preheat the oven to 350°F. Remove the pigs' feet from the broth with a slotted spoon. (Reserve the broth for cooking greens or vegetables.) Arrange them side by side in 2 baking pans large enough to hold them in a single layer. Spoon the barbecue sauce over them and bake 15 minutes. Reduce the heat to 300°F and continue cooking until tender, about 35 minutes.

■ ■ ■

Fish
and Game

Baked Shad with Crabmeat–Corn Bread Stuffing

MAKES 6 SERVINGS

1 recipe Crabmeat–Corn
Bread Stuffing (page 67)
1 whole shad (3 to 4 pounds),
cleaned and butterflied (see
the Note)
4 tablespoons (½ stick)
unsalted butter, melted

2 teaspoons salt
2 teaspoons freshly ground
black pepper
½ cup fresh or dry bread
crumbs

1. Make the Corn Bread Stuffing.
2. Wipe the cleaned shad inside and out with damp paper towels and pat dry. Take a look at the opening along the stomach side of the fish. If necessary, use a small sharp knife to extend the cut so it runs the length of the body cavity—you want to fit as much stuffing in the fish as possible. Brush the cavity and outside of the shad with melted butter. In a small bowl combine the salt and pepper. Sprinkle well over the inside and the skin of the shad.
3. Preheat the oven to 350°F. Place the shad into a well-buttered baking dish. Carefully spoon the corn bread stuffing into the cavity. Don't pack the stuffing too tightly—it will expand a little during cooking. Lightly press the sides of the shad together; skewer with toothpicks to enclose the stuffing. Pat the bread crumbs onto the surface of the fish. Place in the oven and bake until the fish is cooked through at the thickest part and the dressing is heated through, about 40 minutes. To serve, cut a cross section of the fish that contains some stuffing for each person.

Note: Your fishmonger can butterfly the shad for you, or here's how to do it yourself: First, from the head to the tail, extend the cut used to clean the fish so the fish is open like a book, with the skin sides lying flat on the counter. Remove the bones while leaving the fillets attached and joined along where the backbone was.

Crabmeat–Corn Bread Stuffing

MAKES ENOUGH STUFFING FOR ONE 4-POUND SHAD

- 2 cups yellow cornmeal
- ½ cup all-purpose flour
- 2 tablespoons sugar
- 1 tablespoon baking powder
- 1 teaspoon salt
- 2 large eggs, lightly beaten
- 1 cup milk
- ½ cup solid vegetable shortening, melted, plus more for the pan
- 2 green bell peppers, cored, seeded, and finely chopped
- 2 medium onions, finely chopped
- 2 stalks celery, finely chopped
- ½ pound lump crabmeat, picked over for shell and cartilage

1. Preheat the oven to 375°F. Combine the cornmeal, flour, sugar, baking powder, and salt in a large mixing bowl and stir well. Make a well in the center of the dry ingredients and add the eggs, milk, and shortening. Stir together just until the mixture is smooth and blended. Fold in the green peppers, onions, celery, and crabmeat. Spoon the mixture into a well-greased 9-inch square baking pan. Smooth the top with a spatula.

2. Bake until the edges are lightly browned and pull away from the sides of the pan and the center feels firm but moist, about 40 minutes. Let the corn bread cool on wire racks 10 minutes.

3. Turn the corn bread into a bowl and crumble it with two forks.

■ ■ ■

Seafood Gumbo

MAKES 8 SERVINGS

Although the list of ingredients is long, this is a pretty simple dish to put together and well worth the effort. It's a great dish for a special party or a family get-together.

2 quarts beef stock OR canned beef broth
1 cup chopped smoked ham
2 bay leaves
2 tablespoons crushed red pepper flakes
1 tablespoon salt
⅓ cup bacon drippings
⅓ cup all-purpose flour
3 tablespoons vegetable oil
3 cups chopped fresh okra (or frozen, thawed)
2 large onions, chopped
1 green bell pepper, cored, seeded, and minced
2 stalks celery, chopped
2 cloves garlic, minced
1 16-ounce can whole tomatoes

¼ cup catsup
1 tablespoon hot pepper sauce
1 tablespoon Worcestershire sauce
½ teaspoon dried thyme
1 pound shrimp
1 pound crabmeat OR 6 hard-shell crabs, cooked and cleaned
1 bunch scallions, chopped
12 oysters, shucked with liquid OR 1 12-ounce jar oysters, drained
1 cup cooked rice, plus more for serving
1 tablespoon gumbo filé

1. Combine the stock, ham, bay leaves, red pepper, and 2 teaspoons of the salt in a large kettle. Heat to boiling over high heat. Reduce the heat to a simmer, cover, and cook 1 hour.
2. Meanwhile, make the roux: Heat the bacon drippings in a skillet over medium heat. Stir in the flour until absorbed. Cook over very low heat, stirring constantly, until the flour is dark brown and the

roux smells nutty, about 25 minutes. Be careful not to burn the flour or the roux is ruined.

3. In a separate large skillet, heat the oil over medium heat. Add the okra, onions, green peppers, celery, and garlic. Sauté until almost tender, about 10 minutes. Add the tomatoes and cook 5 minutes longer.

4. Add the sautéed vegetables and the roux to the hot beef stock along with remaining 1 teaspoon of salt, the catsup, hot pepper sauce, Worcestershire sauce, and thyme. Reduce the heat to very low and simmer, covered, 1 hour.

5. Stir the shrimp, crabmeat, and scallions into the gumbo. Cook 10 minutes. Add the oysters, rice, and gumbo filé and cook 10 minutes. Check the seasoning and serve over rice.

Note: The recipe can be prepared through Step 4 up to 1 day in advance. Reheat the liquid and finish the recipe just before serving.

■ ■ ■

Fried Catfish

MAKES 4 SERVINGS

Firm, sweet, and juicy catfish fillets are becoming more and more popular with home cooks. Now that they are being farmed commercially they are even easier to find. At Sylvia's, catfish is seasoned and coated with cracker meal before being quickly fried. Serve fried catfish with tartar sauce, Southern Hush Puppies (page 111), and Coleslaw (page 105).

2 **pounds catfish fillets, about ½ inch thick**
1 **teaspoon garlic powder**
2 **teaspoons salt**
½ **teaspoon freshly ground black pepper**

2 **cups cracker meal OR coarsely crushed unsalted crackers**
1 **cup vegetable oil**

1. Trim the catfish of any skin or membrane. Stir the garlic powder, salt, and pepper together in a small bowl. Sprinkle the mixture over both sides of the fillets. Dredge the fillets in the cracker meal, pressing gently so the meal sticks to both sides of the fillets. Shake off the excess and set the fillets aside.

2. Heat the oil in a large heavy skillet over medium heat until a little cracker meal sprinkled in the oil gives off a lively sizzle. Slip the fillets into the skillet and fry, turning once, until the fillets are cooked through and golden brown on both sides, about 8 minutes. Remove and drain on paper towels before serving.

■ ■ ■

Rabbit, Flavored and Fried

MAKES 4 SERVINGS

Cooking times for rabbit can vary greatly. Be sure to test for tenderness as described in the recipe before cooling and frying. Serve this instead of fried chicken for a delicious change.

1 2½- to 3-pound rabbit, cut in 8 pieces (see the Note)	½ teaspoon garlic powder All-purpose flour as
2 teaspoons salt	needed
½ teaspoon freshly ground black pepper	1 cup vegetable oil

1. Cook the rabbit pieces in a 4-quart saucepan of simmering salted water until tender when poked with a fork. This can take anywhere from 10 to 25 minutes. Drain and cool the pieces to room temperature.

2. Mix the salt, pepper, and garlic powder in a small bowl and rub the mixture into the cooled rabbit pieces. Dredge the pieces lightly in flour and shake off the excess.

3. Heat the oil in a large heavy skillet. Add the rabbit pieces and fry, turning as necessary, until golden brown and crispy outside and no trace of pink remains in the center, about 12 minutes for the larger pieces and less for the thinner pieces. Remove and drain briefly before serving.

Note: Whether you are buying fresh rabbit from a butcher, or are dressing your own, the rabbit should be cut into 8 pieces as follows: Cut each of the 2 hind legs into 2 pieces at the joint. Separate the saddle (center portion) from the forelegs and cut the saddle in half through the backbone. Leave the forelegs uncut. Rabbit already cut into serving pieces is available frozen in some areas. Look for rabbit cut into 8 pieces; if it is not available, adapt the cooking time as necessary to suit smaller or larger pieces.

Hash Venison

MAKES 8 SERVINGS

3 to 4 pounds venison, on the bone (see the Note)
1 teaspoon plus 1 tablespoon vegetable oil
8 ounces slab bacon, cut into 4 thick slices
2 cups water, plus more as needed
4 medium onions, finely chopped (about 3 cups)

4 green bell peppers, cored, seeded, and finely chopped (about 3 cups)
2 tablespoons salt
1½ tablespoons freshly ground black pepper
About 1 cup Barbecue Sauce (page 59)

1. Rinse the venison under cold water and pat dry with paper towels. Heat 1 teaspoon of the oil in a 6-quart pot over medium heat. Add the bacon and cook, stirring occasionally, until the bacon has rendered most of its fat, about 10 minutes. Add 2 cups of water and stir to dissolve any brown bits that cling to the pan. Add half the onions and half the green peppers, the salt, pepper, and venison. Pour in enough water to cover the venison. Heat to boiling, reduce the heat to a simmer, and cover the pot. Cook until the venison is very tender, about 3 hours.
2. Carefully transfer the venison to a large plate. Strain the cooking liquid and set it aside.
3. Remove the venison from the bone and shred it with two forks, discarding any gristle as you go. Drain the shredded venison well.
4. Heat the 1 tablespoon of vegetable oil in a large heavy skillet over medium heat. Add the remaining onions and green peppers and stir-fry until soft, about 5 minutes. Add the venison and toss to mix with the vegetables. Continue stir-frying the hash, adding the reserved venison broth as necessary, until the vegetables are

tender and the meat is very moist. Stir in enough barbecue sauce to coat the hash, check the seasonings, and serve hot.

Note: Use either a venison ham, or a 3- to 4-pound cut from the back or rib for this recipe. If you're using frozen venison, be sure it is thoroughly defrosted before starting the recipe.

■ ■ ■

Beans, Potatoes, Rice, and Salads

Macaroni and Cheese

MAKES 8 SERVINGS

One of the favorite side dishes at both lunch and dinner at Sylvia's, this is best if made right before serving and eaten piping hot out of the oven. If you'd like to reheat leftover macaroni and cheese, moisten it with a little milk and cover it tightly before reheating.

12 ounces elbow macaroni (¾ box)
 2 large eggs
 3 tablespoons unsalted butter OR margarine
1½ cups milk
 8 ounces grated cheddar cheese (about 2 cups)

1 teaspoon salt
1 teaspoon freshly ground black pepper
1 teaspoon sugar
½ teaspoon yellow food coloring (optional)

1. Preheat the oven to 375°F. Cook the macaroni in a large pot of boiling salted water until tender but not mushy, about 8 minutes. Drain it very well and transfer it to a large mixing bowl.
2. Mix the macaroni with the remaining ingredients, reserving about ¼ cup each of the milk and the cheese. Transfer to an 11-inch oval baking dish. Pour the reserved milk over the top and sprinkle with the reserved cheese.
3. Bake until the top crust is golden brown and the casserole is bubbling, about 25 minutes. Serve hot.

■ ■ ■

Red Rice and Hot Sausage

MAKES 6 SERVINGS

2 tablespoons vegetable or
corn oil
2 pounds smoked hot
sausages, cut into 2-inch
lengths
1 large onion, finely diced
(about 1½ cups)
1 large green bell pepper,
finely diced (about 1 cup)
3 stalks celery, finely diced
(about 1 cup)

4 cups water
1 15-ounce can tomato
sauce
3 tablespoons salt
1 teaspoon freshly ground
black pepper
2 cups converted rice

1. Heat the oil in a heavy 5-quart pot over medium heat. Add the sausage pieces and cook, stirring often, until brown, about 5 minutes. Add the onions, green peppers, and celery. Cook, stirring, 3 minutes. Add the water, tomato sauce, salt, and pepper. Heat to boiling, stir in the rice, and continue stirring until the sausage comes to the top.
2. Reduce the heat to simmering and cook, covered, until the rice is tender, about 20 minutes. Serve hot.

■ ■ ■

Red Beans and Rice

MAKES 8 SERVINGS

1 cup (about 8 ounces) small
   dried red chili beans
5 cups water
1 smoked ham hock
2 tablespoons salt

½ teaspoon crushed red
   pepper flakes
½ teaspoon dried thyme
2 cups converted rice

1. Soak the beans overnight in 5 cups of water in a cool place or in the refrigerator.
2. Drain the beans and place them in a 5-quart pot. Add 4 cups of water, the ham hock, salt, red pepper, and thyme. Heat to boiling, then reduce the heat to a bare simmer. Cover and cook until the beans are almost tender, about 1 hour.
3. Stir 1 cup of water and the rice into the beans. Heat to boiling, reduce the heat to a simmer, and cook, covered, until the rice and beans are tender and the liquid is absorbed, about 25 minutes. Check the seasonings. If you like, you may remove the meat from the ham hock and mix it into the rice. Serve hot.

■ ■ ■

Red Rice

MAKES 8 SERVINGS

Delicious served with Barbecued Short Ribs of Beef (page 61), this rice also reheats very well. When serving it, be sure to scrape out the pot— the rice around the edges and bottom is especially tasty.

2 tablespoons vegetable oil
½ pound smoked ham, off the bone OR smoked slab bacon OR streaky lean bacon, diced (about 2 cups)
2 medium onions, finely diced (about 1 cup)
2 stalks celery, trimmed and finely diced (about 1 cup)
1 large green bell pepper, cored, seeded, and finely diced (about 1 cup)

1 28-ounce can whole tomatoes, with liquid
¾ cup tomato purée
1½ teaspoons salt
1 teaspoon freshly ground black pepper
1 teaspoon chili powder
2 cups long grain rice
Hot sauce to taste

1. Heat the oil in a 4-quart pot over medium heat. Add the ham, onions, celery, and green peppers and cook until the vegetables are wilted. Add the tomatoes, tomato purée, salt, pepper, and chili powder. Lower the heat to simmering and simmer, covered, 30 minutes. Measure the sauce and, if necessary, add enough water to bring the volume to 5 cups.
2. Stir the rice into the liquid and heat to boiling. Reduce the heat to very low and cook, covered, until the rice is tender, about 45 minutes. Stir once or twice during cooking to prevent sticking. Check the seasonings and add hot sauce to taste.

■ ■ ■

Rice and Chitlins Perlow

MAKES 8 SERVINGS

I love serving this dish to a crowd of family and friends just like my mother did at holiday dinners.

1¾ pounds fresh or frozen cleaned pork chitlins (page 18)

4 cups water

2 onions, coarsely chopped

2 green bell peppers, cored, seeded, and coarsely chopped

3 stalks celery, coarsely chopped

1 tablespoon plus 1 teaspoon salt

2 teaspoons freshly ground black pepper

1 tablespoon crushed red pepper flakes

2½ cups raw long grain rice (1 pound)

1. Place the chitlins in a 4-quart saucepan. Add the water, onions, green peppers, celery, salt, black pepper, and red pepper. Cover and heat to boiling over medium heat. Reduce the heat to simmering, cover, and cook 1 hour.

2. Stir in the rice and continue cooking, covered, until the rice and chitlins are tender, about 45 minutes. Taste and adjust the seasonings if necessary.

■ ■ ■

Potato Salad

MAKES 12 SERVINGS

Sometimes Ruth will dress up this delicious potato salad with a little chopped pimiento or hard-boiled egg.

2½ pounds Maine potatoes
2 tablespoons sweet pickle relish
8 ounces Hellmann's mayonnaise
1 stalk celery, finely chopped
1 medium onion, finely chopped

1 green bell pepper, cored, seeded, and chopped
1 tablespoon sugar
1 teaspoon salt
½ teaspoon freshly ground black pepper
Large pinch of cayenne pepper, plus more for garnish

1. Wash the potatoes but don't peel them. Place the potatoes in a large pot with enough water to cover them. Heat to boiling, then reduce the heat to a simmer. Cook the potatoes until they are tender but not mushy, about 30 minutes. Drain them and cool.

2. Peel the potatoes—a butter knife works well. Finely chop the potatoes and place them in a large bowl. Add the remaining ingredients and beat well until blended. The potato salad should be the consistency of a chunky purée. Taste it and add more cayenne, salt, or pepper if necessary. Transfer to a serving bowl and sprinkle lightly with cayenne pepper.

■ ■ ■

Candied Yams

MAKES 8 SERVINGS

2 pounds yams, peeled and sliced ¼ inch thick

1½ cups water

1 teaspoon pure vanilla extract

4 tablespoons (½ stick) unsalted butter OR margarine, softened

½ cup granulated sugar, or more to taste

½ cup light brown sugar, or more to taste

½ teaspoon ground cinnamon

½ teaspoon ground allspice

1 cup raisins

2 cups pineapple chunks

1. Preheat the oven to 400°F. Place the yams in a 12- by 12-inch baking pan. Pour in the water and vanilla. Mix the butter, both sugars, cinnamon, and allspice in a small bowl until blended. Sprinkle this mixture over the yams. Cover the baking pan tightly and bake 45 minutes.

2. Sprinkle the raisins and pineapple chunks over the yams and baste them with the juices in the pan. Cover the yams and continue baking until very tender and the juices are bubbling, about 20 minutes. Serve hot from the pan.

■ ■ ■

Black-eyed Peas

MAKES 8 SERVINGS

1 pound dried black-eyed
peas
1 piece skin from a smoked
ham OR 2 ounces slab
bacon, cut into a small dice
¼ cup pork rib drippings OR
fried chicken drippings OR
bacon drippings

¾ teaspoon salt
¼ teaspoon freshly ground
black pepper
½ teaspoon sugar

1. Pick over the peas to remove the stones and dirt. Rinse the peas well and soak them in cold water for 20 minutes. Drain well.
2. Combine the peas and the remaining ingredients in a large pot. Pour in enough cold water to cover the peas by 1 inch. Heat to simmering and cook, covered, until the peas are tender but not mushy, about 1½ hours. Keep an eye on the peas while they are cooking and add more water to keep them covered if necessary.

■ ■ ■

Cowpeas and Rice

MAKES 8 SERVINGS

Cowpeas, otherwise known as field peas, are small and round and marked with a distinctive black dot. If you cannot find cowpeas, substitute navy beans, which are similar in size and texture.

1 cup (about ½ pound) dried cowpeas or field peas	1 teaspoon sugar
5 cups water	1 tablespoon salt
½ pound slab bacon, cut into 1-inch cubes	1 teaspoon freshly ground black pepper
	3 cups long grain rice

1. Pick over the cowpeas, discarding any damaged beans and debris. Soak the cowpeas in 5 cups of water overnight in a cool place or in the refrigerator.

2. Drain the cowpeas and place them in a 4-quart pot. Add 4 cups of water, the bacon, sugar, salt, and pepper. Cover and heat to boiling. Reduce to a simmer and cook, covered, until the peas are almost tender, about 1 hour.

3. Stir 1 cup of water and the rice into the peas and simmer, covered, until the rice and peas are tender and most of the liquid is absorbed, about ½ hour. Stir once or twice during cooking. Check the seasonings and serve hot.

■ ■ ■

Pinto Beans with Ham Hocks

MAKES 8 SERVINGS

1 pound dried pinto beans
2 ham hocks (about 1 pound)
1 small onion, chopped (about
  ½ cup)
2 tablespoons salt

1 teaspoon freshly ground
  black pepper
1 teaspoon sugar
1 clove garlic, crushed

1. Soak the beans overnight in the refrigerator in enough cold water to cover by 4 inches. Drain them well.
2. Combine the beans, ham hocks, onion, salt, pepper, sugar, and garlic in a large saucepot. Cover with water and bring to a boil. Reduce the heat to simmering and cook, covered, until the beans are tender, about 45 minutes. Check the seasoning and serve the beans hot.

Note: If you like, remove the meat from the ham hocks, pick it free of fat and gristle, and return it to the beans.

■ ■ ■

Butter Beans with Ham Bone and Okra

MAKES 8 SERVINGS

If you find yourself with a leftover bone from a baked ham, it's just the excuse you need to prepare this fine dish of beans and okra.

1 meaty ham bone (about 1½ pounds) OR 3 large smoked ham hocks
3 cups water
1½ pounds fresh butter beans OR 2 16-ounce cans butter beans, drained
2 tablespoons solid vegetable shortening

1 tablespoon sugar
½ pound okra, washed and thinly sliced
1 tablespoon salt
2 teaspoons freshly ground black pepper

1. Put the ham bone and water in a large saucepan. Cover and heat to boiling. Reduce the heat to simmering and cook, covered, 45 minutes. Remove the ham bone from the saucepan. Remove the meat from the bone, finely shred it, and return both the meat and bone to the pan.
2. Wash the butter beans and add them to the saucepan. Heat to simmering, stir in the remaining ingredients, and simmer until the beans and okra are tender, about 25 minutes (or less for canned beans). Discard the ham bone and serve the beans hot.

■ ■ ■

Lima Beans

MAKES 8 SERVINGS

Dried lima beans are one of the staples of soul food. Serve them whenever you would serve black-eyed peas.

1 **pound dried lima beans**
1 **to 2 pieces skin from a
  smoked ham OR a small
  ham bone**
2 **tablespoons bacon
  drippings**

½ **teaspoon sugar**
½ **teaspoon salt**
¼ **teaspoon freshly ground
  black pepper**

1. Pick over the beans to remove the stones and dirt. Rinse the beans well and drain them. Cover them with cold water and soak them 15 to 20 minutes. Drain well.
2. Combine the beans and all the remaining ingredients in a large pot. Add enough cold water to cover by 1 inch. Heat to simmering and cook, covered, until the beans are tender but not mushy, about 1 hour and 45 minutes. Keep an eye on the beans while they are cooking and add more water to keep the beans covered if necessary. Discard the ham skin and serve hot.

■ ■ ■

Pineapple Salad

MAKES 12 SERVINGS

1 large pineapple
2 8-ounce cans sauerkraut, drained
2 red apples, cored and diced
12 ounces sliced Canadian bacon, cut into thin strips
⅔ cup Hellmann's mayonnaise
½ cup sour cream OR heavy cream

¼ cup lemon juice
2 tablespoons freshly chopped or 1 tablespoon dried dill
2 teaspoons sugar
1 teaspoon salt
½ teaspoon dried rosemary Romaine OR green leaf OR butter lettuce leaves

1. Cut the top of the pineapple off and remove the skin. Cut it into quarters and cut away the core. Cut the pineapple into 1-inch cubes. Toss the pineapple, sauerkraut, apples, and bacon in a bowl.
2. Make the dressing in a separate bowl: Stir together the mayonnaise, sour cream, lemon juice, dill, sugar, salt, and rosemary until blended.
3. To serve, line serving plates or bowls with lettuce leaves. Top with the pineapple mixture and drizzle some of the dressing over each serving.

■ ■ ■

Vegetables and Greens

Fried Green Tomatoes

MAKES 6 SERVINGS

When you use bacon drippings for frying it's best to strain them through a very dry, fine sieve first. If, after straining, you come up short, you can add vegetable oil to make up the difference. Fried green tomatoes are great over grits for breakfast or as a side dish at lunch or dinner.

3 large green or slightly ripe
tomatoes
Salt
Freshly ground black
pepper
About 1 cup fine yellow
cornmeal OR all-purpose
flour

½ cup bacon drippings OR
vegetable oil OR a
mixture of both

1. Slice the tomatoes ¼ inch thick. Sprinkle both sides with salt and pepper. Dredge the tomato slices in the cornmeal until completely coated. Let them dry on a wire rack, 5 to 10 minutes.

2. Heat the bacon drippings in a large heavy skillet over medium heat until an edge of a tomato slice dipped in them gives off a lively sizzle. Carefully slip as many of the tomato slices into the skillet as will fit without crowding. You may have to fry the slices in batches. Fry them, turning them once, until they are golden brown on both sides and tender, about 5 minutes. Remove them to paper towels to drain and repeat with the remaining slices.

■ ■ ■

Stewed Tomatoes and Okra

MAKES 6 SERVINGS

2 large ripe tomatoes (about 1 pound)	¼ cup bacon drippings
1 pound fresh okra	2 teaspoons sugar
2 cups water	2 teaspoons salt
1 medium onion, chopped	1 teaspoon freshly ground black pepper

1. Heat a 4-quart pot of water to boiling. Cut the cores from the tomatoes and cut a small x in the end opposite the core. Add the tomatoes to the boiling water and cook until the skins become loose, about 30 seconds. Drain the tomatoes, cool them under cold running water, and drain them thoroughly. Peel them and cut them in 1-inch pieces.

2. Rinse the okra thoroughly under cold running water. Remove the stems and cut the okra into ½-inch slices. Combine the okra, tomatoes, and the remaining ingredients in a 4-quart pot. Heat to boiling, reduce the heat, and simmer, covered, until the okra is tender, about 30 minutes. Check the seasoning and adjust if necessary.

■ ■ ■

Tomato Okra Gumbo

MAKES 8 SERVINGS

1 beef short rib (about ½ pound) OR 1 pound meaty beef bones
Skin and meat from shank end of a smoked ham OR 1 ham bone
1 small onion, chopped
1 stalk celery, chopped
1 small green bell pepper, cored, seeded, and chopped
1 12-ounce can whole tomatoes
1 12-ounce can tomato purée
1 10-ounce box frozen whole corn kernels, defrosted

1 9-ounce box frozen okra, defrosted
2 tablespoons bacon drippings
2 teaspoons salt
1 teaspoon freshly ground black pepper
1 teaspoon crushed red pepper flakes
¼ cup all-purpose flour
½ cup water

1. Combine the short rib, ham, onions, celery, and green peppers in a large pot. Add enough cold water to cover and heat to boiling. Reduce the heat and simmer until the meat is tender, about 2 hours (or 1½ hours if using beef bones).

2. Add the tomatoes and tomato purée. Heat to boiling. Stir in the corn, okra, bacon drippings, salt, black pepper, and red pepper. Reduce the heat and simmer 20 minutes.

3. Stir the flour into the ½ cup of water until smooth. Slowly pour the flour mixture into the gumbo, stirring constantly until the gumbo is smooth and thickened. Check the seasonings and adjust them if necessary.

■ ■ ■

Mamma's Country Fried Okra

MAKES 6 SERVINGS

1 pound young okra	2 teaspoons freshly ground
½ cup vegetable oil	black pepper, or to taste
2 teaspoons salt, or to taste	

1. Wash the okra in cold water and drain. Cut it into ½-inch slices and remove the stems.

2. Heat half the oil in a large heavy skillet over medium heat. Add half the okra and spread it into an even layer with a spatula. Sprinkle with salt and pepper. Fry, turning the okra with a spoon to cook evenly, until the okra is tender, crispy, and well browned, about 10 minutes. Drain on paper towels. Repeat with remaining oil and okra and serve hot.

New York–Style Fried Okra

After washing and draining the okra, cut it crosswise into 1-inch slices. Beat 3 eggs with a few drops of water in a bowl. Pour some cracker meal into a second bowl. Dredge the sliced okra first in the cracker meal, then coat with the beaten egg. Drain well and coat with cracker meal. The okra is then ready for frying.

■ ■ ■

Fried Yellow Squash with Bacon and Onions

MAKES 6 SERVINGS

2 to 3 pounds yellow squash
½ pound bacon
1 cup yellow cornmeal
½ cup all-purpose flour
1 tablespoon salt

1 teaspoon freshly ground
black pepper
2 medium onions, cut in
half and thinly sliced

1. Slice the squashes on an angle ½ inch thick. Fry the bacon in a large heavy skillet over medium heat until crisp. Remove the bacon and reserve the drippings in the skillet off the heat. Stir the cornmeal, flour, salt, and pepper together in a bowl.
2. Dredge the sliced squash in the cornmeal mixture. Return the skillet of drippings to medium heat. Fry the squash slices in batches until golden brown, about 2 minutes on each side. Remove the fried squash and drain.
3. When all the squash is fried, pour off all but 2 tablespoons of the drippings from skillet. Add the onion slices and cook until tender and lightly browned, about 5 minutes.
4. Place the squash on a serving platter, top with the onions, and crumble the bacon over both.

■ ■ ■

Boiled String Beans with Ham

MAKES 8 SERVINGS

The way most people prepare vegetables nowadays is more like dipping them in boiling water than really cooking them. These beans, which are simmered in a ham broth until tender and very flavorful, are a real treat. Fresh green peas are delicious cooked the same way—reduce the cooking time to about 10 minutes.

1 **bone from a smoked ham**
   OR **8 pigs' tails**
2 **to 3 pounds fresh string
   beans**
1 **tablespoon salt**

1 **teaspoon freshly ground
   black pepper**
1 **teaspoon sugar**

1. Put the ham bone in a 6-quart pot with enough water to fill halfway. Heat to boiling, lower the heat to a simmer, and cover. Simmer 45 minutes.

2. Prepare the beans while the bone is simmering. Snap the stem end from each bean and pull gently along the length of the bean to remove the string. (It may not be necessary to remove the string from very young beans.) Rinse the beans in a colander under cold running water. Drain and add to the pot along with the salt, pepper, and sugar. Simmer the beans until very tender, up to 30 minutes for old tough beans or around 15 minutes for very tender young beans. Check the seasoning halfway through the cooking and adjust if necessary. Remove the bone and drain the beans. Serve hot.

▪ ▪ ▪

Succotash

MAKES 8 SERVINGS

To many people succotash means a lima bean and corn stew. In my delicious version a medley of vegetables are simmered in a rich smoked turkey broth and produce a dish that's almost wet enough to be called a soup.

4 smoked turkey wings
  (about 1¼ pounds) OR an
  equal amount of smoked
  turkey neck bones
6 cups water
1 pound fresh string beans
1 medium onion, chopped
  (about 1 cup)
  Salt to taste
  Freshly ground black
  pepper to taste

6 small new potatoes
  (about 1 pound), washed
  and cut into quarters
¾ pound okra, trimmed
  and sliced ½ inch thick
  OR 1 10-ounce package
  frozen sliced okra,
  defrosted
1 cup frozen corn kernels
  OR corn cut from 4 cobs

1. Put the turkey wings and water in a 5-quart pot. Cover and heat to boiling. Reduce the heat to simmering and cook, covered, for 1½ hours.
2. Meanwhile, wash the string beans, snap off the ends, and pull gently along the lengths to remove the strings. Break each bean into 3 pieces.
3. Add the beans, onions, salt, and pepper to taste to the pot. Simmer, covered, 20 minutes. Add the potatoes, okra, and corn. Simmer until the potatoes are tender, about 15 minutes. Check the seasoning. Serve hot.

■ ■ ■

Corn Pudding

MAKES 8 SERVINGS

Corn oil
2 large eggs
1 6-ounce can evaporated
  milk
¼ cup sugar
1 tablespoon cornstarch
1 16-ounce can creamed corn

1 teaspoon salt
¼ teaspoon freshly ground
  black pepper
1 tablespoon unsalted
  butter OR margarine

1. Lightly grease a 7- by 7-inch baking dish with corn oil. Preheat the oven to 350°F.

2. Beat the eggs and evaporated milk in a small bowl until blended. Stir the sugar and cornstarch together in a small bowl and add them slowly to the egg mixture, beating constantly, until blended. Fold in the corn, salt, and pepper. Pour the mixture into the greased baking dish and dot with the butter.

3. Bake until the pudding is set and golden brown on top, about 1 hour. Serve hot from the dish.

■ ■ ■

Collard Greens

MAKES 6 SERVINGS

Fresh or smoked ham hocks make a good substitute for the skin and bone called for in this recipe. (Use about 1½ pounds for the amount of water given here.) Boiled collards go well with all kinds of foods—from fried chicken to chitlins and meat loaf—and are one of the staples of soul food cooking.

Pork skin and bone from
1 fresh or smoked ham
4 cups water
2 pounds collard greens
1 tablespoon salt

1½ teaspoons crushed red
pepper flakes
1 tablespoon sugar
¼ cup bacon drippings

1. Put the pork skin and bone into a 5-quart pot with the water. Heat to boiling, then reduce to a simmer. Cover the pot and simmer 45 minutes. Skim the foam from the broth once or twice.
2. Meanwhile, prepare the collards: Cut away the very thick part of the stems. Wash the collard greens thoroughly—they can be very gritty. Drain them by shaking off any excess water and chop them into small pieces. Stir the collard greens into the pot and add the salt, red pepper, and sugar. Drizzle all with the bacon drippings. Cook, covered, at a lively simmer until the collard greens are tender, about 20 minutes.
3. Turn off the heat and check the seasonings. Cover the pot and let the collard greens sit a few minutes before serving.

■ ■ ■

Collard Greens with Cornmeal Dumplings

MAKES 8 SERVINGS

Cooking hearty cornmeal dumplings in the pot along with greens gives them an unusual and delicious flavor. It also yields two side dishes from the same pot. Be sure to serve the dumplings as soon as they are cooked.

1 recipe Collard Greens
(page 98)
4 cups water
1 cup cornmeal

½ cup all-purpose flour
1 teaspoon baking powder
1 teaspoon salt
⅔ cup cold milk

1. Prepare the greens according to the recipe, but use an additional 4 cups of water for cooking.
2. Prepare the dumpling mix: Combine the cornmeal, flour, baking powder, and salt and stir well. Pour the milk over the dry ingredients and stir until just moistened.
3. Add the greens to the liquid, cover, and boil 5 minutes.
4. Remove the cover from the greens and drop the dumpling mixture by the heaping teaspoonful over the collards, leaving some space between the dumplings. Cover the pot and continue cooking until the dumplings are cooked through and the greens are tender, about 20 minutes. Be sure to keep the heat at a bare simmer while the dumplings are cooking or they will break apart. Serve the dumplings separately, with some of the pot liquid spooned over them.

■ ■ ■

Collard Greens and Turnips

MAKES 8 SERVINGS

The season for turnips and collard greens runs straight through Christmas, when most other vegetables have long since given up. A plate of piping hot turnips and collard greens will warm up any cold fall or winter day. As with chitlins (page 18), make a big batch of these—the leftovers will disappear fast or they can be frozen.

1½ **pounds meaty ham bone AND/OR skin**
8 **cups water, or as needed**
2½ **pounds fresh turnips, including the greens**
4 **pounds fresh collard greens**
⅓ **cup sugar**

3 **tablespoons salt**
2 **teaspoons freshly ground black pepper**
2 **teaspoons crushed red pepper flakes**
½ **cup bacon drippings**

1. Put the ham bone (and skin) and water in a large pot. Bring to a boil over medium-high heat. Reduce the heat to simmering and cook, covered, 1 hour, or until 2 cups of the liquid is left. Remove from the heat and reserve.

2. Cut the greens from the turnips and reserve. Wash and peel the turnips and slice them about ½ inch thick. Add the sliced turnips to the pot. Heat to boiling over medium heat, cover the pot, and cook 10 minutes. Meanwhile, pick over the reserved turnip greens and the collard greens and cut away any yellow or wilted leaves. Wash the greens thoroughly, drain, and shake out any excess water. Cut away the very thick part of the stems and chop the greens coarsely.

3. Add the chopped greens to the pot along with the sugar, salt, black pepper, and red pepper. Pour the bacon drippings over the top, cover, and cook over medium heat, 25 minutes. Reduce the heat to simmering and cook 10 minutes longer. Remove from the heat, adjust the seasonings, and let stand a few minutes before serving.

■ ■ ■

Mustard Greens and Ham Hocks

MAKES 6 SERVINGS

2 pounds mustard greens OR
  collard greens
1 2-pound green cabbage
3 smoked ham hocks (about 2
  pounds)
3 quarts water
1 tablespoon salt

1 teaspoon freshly ground
  black pepper
1 teaspoon sugar
1 teaspoon thyme leaves
4 medium Idaho potatoes
  (about 2 pounds), peeled
  and cut into quarters

1. Wash the greens thoroughly and drain them by shaking off any excess water. Remove the very thick part of the stems from the greens and coarsely chop the leaves. Cut the cabbage into quarters and cut out the core from the cabbage pieces. Coarsely chop the cabbage and set aside.

2. Put the ham hocks and enough cold water to cover them in a 4-quart saucepan over high heat. Heat to boiling, reduce the heat to simmering, and cook the hocks, covered, until almost tender, about 1½ hours.

3. Stir in the chopped greens, salt, pepper, sugar, and thyme. Cook 30 minutes. Add the cabbage and potatoes and cook until all vegetables are tender, about 30 minutes. Check the seasonings and serve hot.

■ ■ ■

Steamed Cabbage with Butter

MAKES 4 SERVINGS

1 3-pound green cabbage
4 tablespoons (½ stick)
   unsalted butter
½ cup water

1 teaspoon sugar
1 tablespoon salt
½ teaspoon freshly ground
   black pepper

1. Cut the cabbage into quarters. Remove any wilted and discol-ored outer leaves and cut out the core from the cabbage pieces. Cut the cabbage into a large (1-inch) dice.
2. Heat the butter and water to simmering in a 4-quart pot. Stir in the cabbage, sugar, salt, and pepper. Cover the pot and cook the cabbage, stirring occasionally, until the cabbage is tender, about 25 minutes.

■ ■ ■

Fried Cabbage and Bacon

MAKES 6 SERVINGS

1 3-pound green cabbage
½ pound sliced bacon
½ cup water
1 tablespoon sugar

1 tablespoon salt
½ teaspoon freshly ground
black pepper

1. Cut the cabbage into quarters. Remove any wilted and discolored outer leaves and cut out the core from the cabbage pieces. Cut the cabbage into a large (1-inch) dice.

2. Cook the bacon in a 4-quart pot over medium heat until crisp. Remove the bacon to paper towels to drain. There should be about ½ cup bacon drippings in the pan. Add the cabbage to these drippings and cook without stirring until it begins to brown, about 3 minutes. Add the water, sugar, salt, and pepper and cook covered until the cabbage is tender, about 20 minutes. Crumble the cooked bacon into the cabbage and serve hot.

■ ■ ■

Coleslaw

MAKES 6 CUPS

1 2½-pound green cabbage	3 tablespoons sugar
2 large carrots (about ¾ pound)	1 tablespoon prepared mustard
1 cup Hellmann's mayonnaise	1 cup raisins
¼ cup white vinegar, or more or less to taste	

1. Trim the tough outer leaves from the cabbage. Cut the cabbage into quarters and cut away the core from the cabbage pieces. Finely shred the cabbage. There should be about 8 cups. Peel the carrots and trim the ends. Grate them on the coarse side of a grater.

2. Stir the mayonnaise, vinegar, sugar, and mustard together in a large bowl until blended. Add the cabbage, carrots, and raisins and toss to coat with the dressing. Let stand, tossing occasionally, about 15 minutes. Store, covered, in the refrigerator for at least a few hours and toss well before serving.

■ ■ ■

Breads and Biscuits

Cracklin' Corn Bread

MAKES 8 SERVINGS

This is corn bread died and gone to heaven—made rich with crunchy pork cracklin's and sweetened with cane syrup.

Butter OR solid vegetable shortening, softened
1 cup pork cracklin's
3 cups yellow cornmeal
2 cups all-purpose flour
¼ cup sugar
2 tablespoons baking powder

2 teaspoons salt
1½ cups milk
1 cup cane syrup
¾ cup solid vegetable shortening, melted
4 large eggs, lightly beaten

1. If necessary, make the cracklin's (see the Note). Preheat the oven to 350° F. Lightly grease a 13- by 9- by 2-inch baking dish with the butter or shortening.
2. Stir the cornmeal, flour, sugar, baking powder, and salt in a large mixing bowl until well combined.
3. Beat the milk, syrup, shortening, and eggs in a separate bowl until blended. Pour the wet ingredients over the dry ingredients, add the cracklin's, and stir until just blended—a few lumps won't matter.
4. Pour the batter into the prepared baking dish and bake until the edges are light brown and pull away from the sides of the baking dish, about 35 to 40 minutes. Cool on a wire rack 20 minutes before serving.

Note: To make cracklin's, cut the pork skin with attached fat into ½-inch pieces. Combine the pork skin pieces and ¼ cup water in a large heavy skillet (cast-iron is perfect) over medium heat. When the water comes to a boil, reduce the heat to very low. Stir occasionally to keep the pieces from sticking until all the fat has been rendered and the pieces of skin are brown and very crisp. Keep the heat low to prevent the fat from browning. Strain the fat and drain the cracklin's briefly on paper towels. This strained rendered fat is lard and can be used for many dishes. Any unused cracklin's can be set aside and used in bean and vegetable dishes.

■ ■ ■

Corn Bread

MAKES 8 SERVINGS

Butter OR solid vegetable shortening, softened
1⅓ cups cornmeal
1 cup all-purpose flour
3 tablespoons sugar
1 tablespoon plus 1 teaspoon baking powder

½ teaspoon salt
1 cup milk
½ cup vegetable oil
2 large eggs

1. Preheat the oven to 375° F. Lightly grease an 11- by 8-inch baking pan with the butter or shortening.
2. Stir the cornmeal, flour, sugar, baking powder, and salt in a large bowl until mixed. Beat the milk, oil, and eggs in a separate bowl until blended. Pour the wet ingredients into the center of the dry ingredients and mix with a fork until just blended—a few lumps won't matter.
3. Pour the batter into the prepared pan and bake in the center of the oven until golden brown and the edges begin to pull away from the sides of the pan, about 35 minutes. Remove and cool 5 to 10 minutes before cutting and serving.

Note: Many ovens bake unevenly. Check the corn bread halfway through the baking time and rotate the pan if one side is browning more quickly.

■ ■ ■

Southern Hush Puppies

MAKES ABOUT 20

Hush puppies are a cornmeal fritter, usually deep-fried and served with fried catfish or other fried foods. I came up with this panfried version for the home cook.

2 cups yellow cornmeal
1 cup all-purpose flour
3 tablespoons sugar
2 teaspoons baking powder
2 teaspoons salt
¾ cup milk
2 large eggs, well beaten

1½ teaspoons plus ¼ cup vegetable oil
2 medium onions, finely chopped (about 1 cup)
1 green bell pepper, cored, seeded, and finely chopped (about 1 cup)

1. Combine the cornmeal, flour, sugar, baking powder, and salt in a bowl and stir until thoroughly blended. Make a well in the center of the dry ingredients and add the milk, eggs, and 1½ teaspoons of the oil. Stir the dry ingredients into the wet ingredients until just moistened. Add the onions and green peppers and stir until just blended.
2. Pour the remaining ¼ cup of vegetable oil into a large skillet over medium heat. Using a tablespoon, form the batter into half-dollar-size cakes and fry, turning once, until golden brown on both sides, about 5 minutes. Drain on paper towels.

■ ■ ■

Banana Nut Bread

MAKES 1 LOAF

8 tablespoons (1 stick) unsalted butter, softened, plus more for the pan
2 cups all-purpose flour, plus more for the pan
1 tablespoon baking powder
½ teaspoon ground nutmeg

¼ teaspoon salt
2 large ripe bananas, peeled
1 teaspoon vanilla extract
½ cup sugar
1 large egg
½ cup raisins
½ cup chopped pecans

1. Preheat the oven to 350°F. Butter and flour a 9- by 5- by 3-inch loaf pan.

2. Sift the 2 cups of flour, baking powder, nutmeg, and salt into a bowl. Mash the bananas with the vanilla with a potato masher until smooth. Cream the 8 tablespoons of butter and sugar in a separate mixing bowl until light and fluffy. Add the egg and beat until well blended. Add the dry ingredients to the butter mixture alternately with the mashed banana, raisins, and pecans, beginning and ending with the dry ingredients. Spoon the batter into the prepared pan, smoothing the top. Bake until golden brown and a cake tester inserted in the center comes out clean, about 1 hour. Let cool 10 minutes before removing from the pan.

■ ■ ■

Blueberry Bread

MAKES 1 LOAF

1 tablespoon plus 8 tablespoons (1 stick) unsalted butter, softened

2½ cups plus 2 tablespoons cake flour

1 tablespoon baking powder

½ teaspoon salt

1 cup sugar

2 large eggs

1 teaspoon vanilla extract

½ cup milk

2 cups blueberries

1. Preheat the oven to 350°F. Grease a 9- by 5- by 3-inch loaf pan, using 1 tablespoon of the butter.

2. Sift 2½ cups of the flour, the baking powder, and salt into a bowl. In a separate bowl, cream the 8 tablespoons butter and the sugar until light and fluffy. Add the eggs one at a time, beating well after each. Beat in the vanilla. Add the sifted dry ingredients and the milk to the butter mixture alternately in 3 batches. Toss the blueberries in a bowl with the remaining 2 tablespoons of flour and fold them into the batter.

3. Turn the batter into the prepared pan and bake until a cake tester inserted into the center comes out clean, about 1 hour and 10 minutes.

■ ■ ■

Desserts

Peach Cobbler

MAKES 12 SERVINGS

Ruth spends most of her mornings putting together enormous cobblers that disappear as soon as she can bake them. This recipe, adapted for a home-size baking pan, can satisfy your craving for Southern-style peach cobbler if you can't make it to see Sylvia.

3 29-ounce cans cling peach halves, drained	2 tablespoons vanilla extract
1½ cups plus 2 tablespoons sugar	⅓ cup all-purpose flour
¾ cup (1½ sticks) plus 2 tablespoons unsalted butter	¾ cup water
	1 recipe Biscuits (page 2)

1. Combine the peaches, 1½ cups of the sugar, ¾ cup of the butter, and the vanilla in a heavy 4-quart pot over medium heat. Heat to simmering and cook until the butter is melted. Stir the flour into the water in a small bowl until smooth. Stir this paste into the peaches. Simmer and stir well, scraping the bottom and sides, until the peach liquid is thickened and smooth, about 3 minutes.

2. Cool the peaches to room temperature, then chill them thoroughly, covered well with plastic wrap.

3. Lightly grease a 13- by 9- by 2-inch baking dish. Heat the oven to 350°F. Prepare the biscuit dough.

4. Roll out two thirds of the dough on a lightly floured surface to a 15- by 19-inch rectangle. Fold the dough in thirds and place it into the baking dish. Unfold the dough and center it in the dish so there is about a 1-inch overhang around all of the edges. Spoon the chilled peach filling onto the dough and smooth the top. Sprinkle with the remaining 2 tablespoons of sugar and dot with the remaining 2 tablespoons of butter. Roll out the remaining biscuit

dough to a 9- by 13-inch rectangle. Cover the peach filling with this dough and fold the overhanging dough over the top piece. Crimp the edges or press them with a fork to seal. Poke the top of the dough with a fork several times.

5. Bake until the filling is set (it will barely jiggle when you tap it with your fingers) and the crust is a deep golden brown. This will take about 1 hour and 50 minutes. Rotate the baking dish once or twice during the cooking if you see that it is cooking unevenly. Remove and cool before serving.

■ ■ ■

Pie Pastry

MAKES ENOUGH FOR A DOUBLE-CRUST 9-INCH PIE

2½ cups sifted all-purpose
   flour
¼ cup sugar
1 teaspoon salt
1 cup solid vegetable
   shortening, chilled

4 tablespoons (½ stick)
   unsalted butter, chilled
   and cut into 8 pieces
1 cup milk

1. Measure the flour, sugar, and salt into a large mixing bowl. Make a well in the center of the dry ingredients and add the shortening and butter. Cut the butter and shortening into the dry ingredients with a pastry blender or 2 butter knives until the mixture is the size of small peas. (Keeping the shortening cold and firm while mixing makes a flakier crust: If the shortening is getting soft at this point, refrigerate the mixture right in the bowl for 5 to 10 minutes.)
2. Sprinkle the milk over the flour mixture and toss with a fork until the pastry is just wet enough to form a crumbly ball. Turn the pastry onto a lightly floured surface and gather it into a ball. Mix the dough quickly with your fingertips until just evenly moist. It's better to leave the pastry a little undermixed and crumbly—overmixing makes a tough dough. Wrap the pastry in waxed paper or paper towels and refrigerate it from 1 hour to overnight.

■ ■ ■

Sweet Potato Pie

MAKES ONE 10-INCH PIE

1 10-inch Pie Shell (page 124)
2½ cups mashed cooked sweet potatoes
8 tablespoons (1 stick) unsalted butter, softened
1¾ cups sugar, or less, to taste

1 teaspoon ground nutmeg
1 teaspoon vanilla extract
2 large eggs
1 7-ounce can evaporated milk

1. Make the pie shell and cool it. Reduce the oven to 300°F.
2. Beat the sweet potatoes and butter with an electric mixer until smooth. Add the sugar, nutmeg, and vanilla and continue beating until incorporated. Add the eggs, one at a time, beating well after each. Add the milk slowly, beating continuously.
3. Transfer the filling to the cool pie shell and smooth the top with a spoon. Bake until the pie is set in the center and lightly browned, about 40 minutes.

■ ■ ■

Apple Pie

MAKES 8 SERVINGS

1 recipe Pie Pastry (page 118)
2 tablespoons lemon juice
12 small tart pie apples (about
   3½ pounds), peeled, cored,
   and each cut into 8 wedges
½ cup brown sugar

2 teaspoons vanilla extract
½ teaspoon cinnamon
½ teaspoon nutmeg
4 tablespoons (½ stick)
   unsalted butter

1. Make the pie pastry and chill it while you're making the filling.
2. Pour the lemon juice into a large mixing bowl. Peel, core, and cut the apples into 8 wedges. Toss the wedges into the lemon juice as you cut them to prevent them from turning brown. When all the apples are peeled and cut, add the brown sugar, vanilla, cinnamon, and nutmeg to the bowl. Toss until the sugar is dissolved and the apples are coated with syrup.
3. Preheat the oven to 375°F. Cut the pastry into two even pieces. Return one half to the refrigerator and roll the other half on a lightly floured surface to an 11-inch circle. The pastry should be about ⅛ inch thick. Fold the circle in half and lift it gently into a 9-inch pie pan. Unfold the pastry and center it in the pan. There should be about 1 inch of pastry overhanging the sides of the pan.
4. Toss the apples in the syrup and spoon the mixture into the pastry-lined pan. Dot with the butter.
5. Roll out the second half of the pastry to an 11-inch circle. Cut 2 or 3 small holes near the center of the pastry. Fold the pastry in half and lift it over the apple filling. Unfold the pastry over the filling, centering it evenly. The edges of the top and bottom pastries should be just about even. Fold the bottom pastry over the top and press it gently to seal. Crimp the pastry around the edge of the pan to form a tight seal.

6. Place the pie on a baking sheet and bake until the crust is golden brown and the apples are soft, about 1 hour. If the edges of the crust are browning faster than the rest of the pie, carefully cover them with strips of aluminum foil to prevent further browning. Cool the pie on a wire rack at least 1 hour before serving.

■ ■ ■

Lemon Meringue Pie

MAKES ONE 10-INCH PIE

1 10-inch Pie Shell (page 124)

LEMON FILLING

½ **cup sugar**
5 **tablespoon cornstarch**
2 **cups cold water**
3 **large eggs, separated (save the whites for the meringue)**
½ **cup freshly squeezed lemon juice**
  Zest from 2 medium-size lemons (about 2 teaspoons)
4 **tablespoons (½ stick) unsalted butter**

NEVER-FAIL MERINGUE

1 **tablespoon cornstarch**
7 **tablespoons sugar**
½ **cup cold water**
3 **egg whites**
½ **teaspoon cream of tartar**
  Pinch of salt
1 **tablespoon vanilla extract**

1. Make the pie shell. When the pie shell is done, increase the oven temperature to 375°F.

2. While the shell is baking, prepare the filling: Combine the sugar and cornstarch in a mixing bowl. Add ½ cup of the water and stir until smooth. Add the egg yolks one at a time, beating well after each. Continue beating until the mixture is pale yellow and fluffy. Add the lemon juice and zest and beat until blended. Gradually beat in the remaining 1½ cups of water. Transfer the mixture to the top of a double boiler over simmering water. Cook, stirring constantly, until the mixture is thick enough to coat a spoon. Remove from the heat and stir in the butter until melted.

3. Make the meringue: In a small saucepan, mix the cornstarch, 1 tablespoon of the sugar, and the cold water. Cook, stirring constantly, over low heat until thick and glossy. Set aside. Whip the egg whites, cream of tartar, and salt in a large bowl until foamy. Slowly add the remaining 6 tablespoons of sugar, one at a time, beating constantly. Add the cornstarch mixture and continue beating until the meringue is very firm. Add the vanilla to meringue.

4. Spoon the lemon filling into the baked pie shell. Smooth into an even layer. Top the filling with the meringue, mounding it high toward the center of the pie. Bake until the meringue is well browned, about 10 minutes. Cool before serving.

■ ■ ■

Pie Shell

MAKES ONE 10-INCH PIE SHELL

2 cups sifted all-purpose
   flour
3 tablespoons sugar
½ teaspoon salt
¾ cup solid vegetable
   shortening, chilled

4 tablespoons (½ stick)
   unsalted butter, chilled
   and cut into 8 pieces
¾ cup plus 1 tablespoon
   milk

1. Measure the flour, sugar, and salt into a large mixing bowl. Make a well in the center of the dry ingredients and add the shortening and butter. Cut the butter and shortening into the dry ingredients with a pastry blender or two butter knives until the mixture is the size of small peas. (Keeping the shortening cold and firm while mixing makes a flakier crust: If the shortening is getting soft at this point, refrigerate the mixture right in the bowl for 5 to 10 minutes.)

2. Sprinkle the milk over the flour mixture and toss with a fork until the pastry is just wet enough to form a crumbly ball. Turn the pastry onto a lightly floured surface and gather it into a ball. Mix the dough quickly with your fingertips until just evenly moist. It's better to leave the pastry a little undermixed and crumbly—overmixing makes a tough dough. Wrap the pastry in waxed paper or paper towels and refrigerate it from 1 hour to overnight.

3. Roll out the pastry on a lightly floured surface to a 13-inch circle. The pastry should be about ⅛ inch thick. Fold the circle in half and lift gently to a 10-inch pie pan. Unfold the pastry and center it in the pan. There should be about 1 inch of pastry overhanging the sides of the pan. Tuck this overhang underneath to form a double thick rim of crust that is even with the edge of the pie pan. Refrigerate the shell, uncovered, 30 minutes to 1 hour.

4. Preheat the oven to 350°F. Line the bottom and sides of the pie shell with aluminum foil. (Allow at least a 1-inch overhang all the way around to make it easier to remove the weights after baking.) Fill the shell halfway with uncooked rice or beans. Bake 15 minutes.
5. Carefully remove the foil and the weights and prick the bottom of the shell with a fork at 1-inch intervals. Return the shell to the oven and continue baking until light golden brown, about 10 minutes. Rotate the shell as necessary to ensure even browning.
6. Remove the shell and cool thoroughly before filling.

■ ■ ■

Three-Layer Caramel Cake

MAKES 12 SERVINGS

2 cups (4 sticks) unsalted
   butter, at room temperature,
   plus more for the pans
3 cups sifted all-purpose
   flour, plus more for the pans
1 tablespoon baking powder
2 cups sugar

2 teaspoons vanilla extract
6 large eggs, at room
   temperature
½ cup milk

Caramel Icing (recipe
   follows)

1. Preheat the oven to 350°F. Lightly grease and flour three 8-inch round cake pans and set aside.
2. Sift the flour and baking powder together and set aside. Cream the butter and sugar in the bowl of an electric mixer at medium speed until the mixture is light and fluffy. Add the vanilla. Beat in the eggs one at a time. Change the mixer speed to low and add the dry ingredients alternately with the milk, a little at a time. Mix just until the ingredients are blended. Overmixing will make the cake layers tough.
3. Divide the batter among the prepared cake pans. Bake until a toothpick inserted into the center of each layer comes out clean, about 20 to 25 minutes. Remove the pans to a wire rack to cool.
4. After about 20 minutes, remove the layers from the pans and let them cool completely on wire racks before frosting.
5. When the layers are completely cool, make the frosting. Place one layer on a plate and spread it with about one fourth of the icing. Top with a second layer and spread it with the same amount of icing. Top with the remaining layer. Frost the top and sides of the cake with the remaining icing. Let the cake set at least ½ hour before serving.

Caramel Icing

MAKES ENOUGH FOR ONE 8-INCH THREE-LAYER CAKE

1 cup (2 sticks) unsalted butter, cut into 8 pieces
1 pound light brown sugar

1 cup granulated sugar
1 12-ounce can evaporated milk

Stir together all the ingredients in a medium heavy saucepan over low heat. Cook, stirring constantly, until the sugars are completely dissolved. Insert a candy or deep-frying thermometer into the icing and boil the icing until the temperature reaches 240°F. This will take about 20 minutes. To test if the icing is ready without a thermometer, drop 1/2 teaspoon of it into a glass of cold water—it's ready if it thickens and forms a soft ball.

Note: Let the icing cool to room temperature, stirring occasionally, until it is thick enough to spread on the cake. If the icing hardens completely, rewarm slowly over low heat. The icing may look a little grainy as it cools—that is normal.

■ ■ ■

Black Rum Cake

MAKES TWO 9-INCH ROUND CAKES OR FOUR 9- BY 5-INCH LOAVES

Rich and dense, loaded with fruit and spiked with rum, this cake is a perfect holiday treat. Prepare the soaked fruit about a month before you plan to bake the cakes, to give it time to mellow. The amount of dried fruit given here is enough for two cakes, but it is easier to prepare the cakes one at a time, adding half the fruit mixture to each. If you plan to bake only one cake, simply prepare half of the fruit mix.

FRUIT MIX (FOR 2 CAKES)

- 2 pounds dark raisins
- 1 pound currants
- 1 pound pitted dried prunes
- ¼ pound glacéed cherries
- ½ pound mixed candied citrus peel (orange, lemon, citron)
- ½ cup dark brown sugar
- 1 cup dark rum, such as Myers's

ONE CAKE

- 1 cup (2 sticks) unsalted butter, softened, plus more for the pan
- 2 cups all-purpose flour
- ½ teaspoon baking powder
- ½ teaspoon salt
- 1½ cups packed dark brown sugar
- 5 large eggs
- 1½ teaspoons vanilla extract
- 1½ teaspoons almond extract
- 1 cup port wine
- ½ cup water
- ¼ cup dark rum
  Butter Icing (recipe follows)

1. Make the soaked fruit mixture at least 3 weeks before baking the cakes: Finely chop the dried and candied fruits. (This can be done in a food processor; first spray the bowl and blade with a nonstick vegetable spray.) Add the sugar and rum to the chopped fruit and store, tightly covered, in a cool place for at least 3 weeks or up to 2 months.

2. Preheat the oven to 300°F. Lightly butter a 9-inch springform pan. Line the bottom with waxed paper and butter the waxed paper.

3. Sift the flour, baking powder, and salt into a large bowl. In a separate bowl, cream the butter and brown sugar with an electric mixer until light and fluffy. Add the eggs one at a time and mix well. Stir in the vanilla and almond extracts. Add the sifted dry ingredients and the port and water to the egg mixture alternately in 3 batches. The batter will have a slightly curdled appearance. Stir in half of the soaked fruit mixture until thoroughly blended.

4. Pour the batter into the buttered cake pan and smooth the top with a spoon. Bake until a cake tester inserted into the center comes out clean, about 2 hours and 40 minutes.

5. Pour the rum over the cake and let the cake cool thoroughly before removing it from the pan. Frost the top and sides of the cake with Butter Icing.

Butter Icing

½ cup (1 stick) unsalted butter, softened
2 cups confectioners' sugar
2 teaspoons vanilla extract

2 tablespoons milk, or more as needed
Few drops of yellow food coloring (if desired)

Cream the butter and sugar until light and fluffy. Beat in the vanilla and 2 tablespoons of milk. The icing should be a smooth spreadable consistency; if not, add more milk a few drops at a time. Beat in the food coloring.

Pound Cake

MAKES 8 SERVINGS

2 cups (4 sticks) unsalted butter, softened, plus more for the pan
3 cups cake flour, plus more for the pan

3½ cups sugar
8 large eggs
1 cup heavy cream OR milk
2 tablespoons vanilla extract

1. Preheat the oven to 350°F. Butter and flour a 9- by 4½-inch loaf pan.

2. Beat the butter in the bowl of an electric mixer until soft. Gradually add the sugar and continue beating at high speed until very light and fluffy. Add the eggs one at a time and beat well after each. When they are thoroughly blended, add the flour 1 cup at a time and beat at low speed until just blended. Stir in the cream and vanilla.

3. Transfer the batter to the loaf pan and bake until golden brown and a cake tester inserted in the center comes out clean, about 1½ hours. Cool 10 minutes, remove the cake from the pan, and cool it completely before serving.

■ ■ ■

Golden Coconut Cake

MAKES ONE 9-INCH THREE-LAYER CAKE, 10 SERVINGS

1 cup (2 sticks) unsalted
   butter, softened, plus 2
   tablespoons for the pans
3 cups sifted cake flour, plus
   more for the pans
1 tablespoon baking powder
¼ teaspoon salt
2 cups sugar

4 large eggs
2 teaspoons vanilla extract
1 cup milk
   Double recipe Butter
   Icing (page 129)
1 cup sweetened coconut
   flakes OR shredded
   coconut, toasted

1. Preheat the oven to 350°F. Butter three 9-inch cake pans with the 2 tablespoons butter and coat them lightly with flour.
2. Sift the flour, baking powder, and salt into a separate bowl. Cream the butter and sugar in a mixing bowl until light and fluffy. Add the eggs one at a time, beating thoroughly after each is added. Stir in the vanilla. Add the dry ingredients and the milk to the butter mixture alternately in 3 batches. Divide the batter evenly among the 3 cake pans. Bake until a cake tester inserted into the center of each layer comes out clean, about 30 minutes. Let the layers cool thoroughly before removing them from the pans and frosting them.
3. Prepare the Butter Icing.
4. Frost the tops of two of the layers and place one on top of the other. Top with the third layer. Frost the top and sides of the cake and decorate the sides of the cake with the coconut. Store, covered, at room temperature until serving.

■ ■ ■

Chocolate Layer Cake

MAKES ONE 8-INCH TWO-LAYER CAKE

1 cup (2 sticks) butter, softened, plus more for the pans

2 cups cake flour, plus more for the pans

1 cup milk

¾ cup unsweetened cocoa, sifted

1 teaspoon baking powder

1 teaspoon baking soda

½ teaspoon salt

1½ cups sugar

8 large eggs

1 tablespoon vanilla extract

1. Preheat the oven to 350°F. Butter and flour 2 round 8-inch cake pans.

2. Heat the milk in a saucepan over medium heat. In a small bowl, carefully whisk the milk into the sifted cocoa to dissolve it without any lumps. Set aside.

3. Sift together the cake flour, baking powder, baking soda, and salt into a bowl. In a separate mixing bowl, cream the butter and sugar until light and fluffy. Add the eggs one at a time, beating well after each. Beat in the vanilla.

4. Add the dry ingredients and cocoa to the creamed butter alternately in 3 batches. Mix well after each addition and scrape down the sides of the bowl.

5. Divide the batter between the cake pans and bake until a cake tester inserted into the center of each layer comes out clean, about 45 minutes. Cool the layers on wire racks for 10 minutes before removing them from the pans.

■ ■ ■

Fresh Peach Cake

MAKES 12 SERVINGS

1 cup (2 sticks) unsalted butter, at room temperature, plus more for the pan

2 cups all-purpose flour, plus more for the pan

1½ cups sugar

3 large eggs

1 teaspoon salt

1 teaspoon baking soda

1 teaspoon cinnamon

2 tablespoons milk

2 cups sliced, peeled fresh peaches OR nectarines (about 4 small peaches) OR 1 16-ounce can sliced peaches, drained

½ cup chopped walnuts OR pecans

1. Preheat the oven to 375°F. Lightly butter and flour a 13- by 9-inch baking dish.

2. Cream the cup of butter and the sugar in a large bowl until light and fluffy. Beat in the eggs one at a time. Continue beating until pale yellow and fluffy. Sift the flour, salt, baking soda, and cinnamon into a separate bowl. Fold the dry ingredients into the egg mixture. Fold in the milk, then fold in the peaches and walnuts. Pour the batter into the baking dish.

3. Bake until a cake tester inserted into the center of the cake comes out clean, about 30 minutes. Cool the cake before slicing it. Serve warm with whipped cream or ice cream.

■ ■ ■

Banana Pudding

MAKES 8 SERVINGS

The only thing better than a freshly baked banana pudding is finding a little leftover piece tucked into the back corner of the icebox—it's delicious chilled, with a cold glass of milk. Use bananas that are perfectly ripe, but not mushy, for this pudding.

2 cups milk
4 tablespoons (½ stick) unsalted butter
1 cup sugar
1 tablespoon vanilla extract
½ teaspoon yellow food coloring (optional)

3 tablespoons cornstarch
½ cup warm water
2 large egg yolks
4 large ripe bananas
About ½ box vanilla wafer cookies

1. Combine the milk, butter, sugar, vanilla, and food coloring in a heavy saucepan. Stir occasionally until the sugar is dissolved and the milk is simmering. Stir the cornstarch and water together in a small bowl until the cornstarch is dissolved. Stir this paste into the milk and simmer, stirring constantly, until thickened. Add the egg yolks and keep stirring constantly, 1 minute. Transfer to a bowl and cool to room temperature. Stir the pudding occasionally while it's cooling to prevent a skin from forming.

2. Preheat the oven to 350°F. Slice 2 of the bananas and arrange the slices in an even layer in the bottom of an 8- by 8-inch baking dish. Cover them with a slightly overlapping layer of about half the vanilla wafers. Spoon half the pudding over the cookies and smooth, pressing the pudding into the layers. Repeat with the remaining bananas, cookies, and pudding. Bake until the top of the pudding is golden brown, about 30 minutes. Cool completely before serving.

■ ■ ■

Berries and Dumplings

MAKES 8 SERVINGS

Whenever we're back home in South Carolina Ruth and I make this dish with brierberries, which resemble large black raspberries. When brierberries aren't available, blueberries make an excellent substitute. If you like, serve this dessert with ice cream or heavy cream.

3 pints brierberries OR
   blueberries
2 quarts water
2½ cups sugar
2 cups all-purpose flour

1 tablespoon baking
   powder
½ teaspoon salt
1 cup milk
   Heavy cream OR vanilla
   ice cream (optional)

1. Combine the berries, water, and sugar in a 4- to 5-quart pot. Bring to a boil over medium heat and let boil 5 minutes. Reduce the heat to simmering.
2. Meanwhile, prepare the dumplings: Sift the flour, baking powder, and salt into a large bowl. Make a well in the center of the flour and slowly pour in the milk while stirring gently with a fork to make a loose semisoft dough. Don't overmix.
3. Gently form the dough into walnut size balls, handling the dough as little as possible. Drop the dumplings gently into the simmering berry liquid. Cover and simmer until a toothpick inserted into the center of the dumplings comes out clean and dry, about 25 minutes. Cool slightly and serve the berries and dumplings warm, with heavy cream or ice cream if you like.

■ ■ ■

Index